May Gibbs

Mother of the Gumnuts

by

Maureen Walsh

SYDNEY UNIVERSITY PRESS

Published by
SYDNEY UNIVERSITY PRESS
University of Sydney Library
www.sup.usyd.edu.au

First published by Angus & Robertson Publishers in 1985

This edition based on the 1994 paperback edition

Sydney University Press
Fisher Library F03
University of Sydney
NSW 2006 AUSTRALIA
Email: info@sup.usyd.edu.au

ISBN 13 978-1-920898-49-6

Typeset by Laserwords Private Limited, Chennai, India

ABOUT THE AUTHOR

Maureen Walsh, a fourth generation Australian, after a background in theatre of the fifties joined the crew of the 'Whiplash' TV Series in 1960 and during the next three decades enjoyed a challenging career in the motion picture industry in North America and Australia. She has screen credits for writing, direction, production and editing for feature films, advertising, industrial films and documentaries.

In 1986 Maureen produced and directed a documentary, 'An Interview with May Gibbs', which won an award in the Biographical Section of the New York International Film and Television Festival. Maureen now enjoys a retired lifestyle in the tropics of Queensland.

The May Gibbs quest has taken up a large portion of Maureen's working and retirement years. With the help of those who care for our heritage, May's memory has been kept alive. Maureen reminisces 'It's hard to say if May found me or I found May and all her little creatures. I certainly grew up on Bib and Bub'.

ACKNOWLEDGEMENTS

May Gibbs' biography grew out of another project undertaken prior to International Women's Year in 1975. May Gibbs was one of six women whose life stories I intended to document on film, an ambitious proposal that was not realised. However, I was extremely surprised that so little had been documented about May Gibbs, an author whose published works were so popular with Australian children, and so, in between assignments, I pursued a number of leads.

Unknown to me I had stepped into what I came to regard as May Gibbs' magic circle, and there was no getting out. Each time my enthusiasm for the project waned, a letter, a telephone call or some incident motivated me to take the next step.

I am indebted to a number of people who had known, visited, worked with and for, or lived with May Gibbs in the latter years of her life. My first lead was Shirley Field who was working as a volunteer with UNICEF, and interviews followed with Carol Odell, Stephen Wilson, Win Raynor, Eric Marden, Len Knight, Win Holden, George Ferguson, John Ferguson, Aubrey Cousins, Beatrice Davis, T. Porter, June Garwood, Mrs C. A. Smith, D. Fenwick, B. Asmus, Ruth Kerr, G. Kendell, G. H. Jarvis, Barbara Haydon Nelson, Judith Wallace, Ruth Trant-Fischer, Mabel King, John Ryan, Peggy Cookson, Nell Couran (Palmer), Florence Carson, D. Philips, Shirley Malcolm, Ron Wright, Angela Epstein, Sydney Nicholls, Maurice Saxby, Hazel de Berg, Beatrice Stavenhagen, John Mitchell, John Baillie and Mrs B. W. Pratt (Pixie O'Harris).

Mrs Pratt directed me to a paper she had written and lodged with the Mitchell Library, Sydney, titled 'A Memory of May Gibbs'. From the staff I learned that artwork and papers from the May Gibbs Estate had been lodged with the Mitchell Library. I convinced Shirley Humphries, the Deputy Mitchell Librarian, of my sincerity in pursuing a work on May Gibbs, and with the Estate's permission twenty-five cardboard cartons, which had held May Gibbs' personal collection since her death, were brought from the Archives. Margaret Collins, with the help of Marian Shand, sorted this abundance. It took two years to catalogue. The Mitchell Library staff have been most supportive and I appreciate their care.

This is my first venture into the literary field and I owe a great deal for help received to Barbara Mobbs, Tim Curnow, Joy Cavill and particularly to my editor Mary Coleman, and Fiona Daniels.

May Gibbs' family have generously allowed me access to correspondence, supplied information and related personal memories of her life. Nephews John and Kenneth Gibbs of Perth and Majorie Ridley of Bunbury, Western Australia, have given invaluable assistance. I am particularly grateful for the help given by the late Josephine Gibbs, May's sister-in-law. It is sad she will not see the end result.

To May Gibbs' most ardent fan, Marian Shand, and her husband Neil I express my sincere thanks. Both have not only given me every support and help but engendered renewed enthusiasm in the project when my spirits were flagging.

The following organisations and their staff have also given their time and help which I acknowledge with thanks: Battye Library, Perth; the Art Gallery of Western Australia, Perth; Bunbury City Council Library, Bunbury; the Art Gallery of South Australia, Adelaide; the State Library of South Australia, Adelaide; Launceston Museum, Launceston; National Library, Canberra; Australian Archives, Canberra; Angus and Robertson Archives, Sydney; Ure Smith, now a division of Landsdowne Press, Sydney; the *Bulletin*, Sydney; the *Sydney Morning Herald*, Sydney; the *Daily Telegraph*, Sydney; the *North Shore Times*, Sydney; the *Weekend Australian*, Sydney; the *News*, Adelaide; the *Sunday Mail*, Adelaide; the *Age*, Melbourne; the *Courier Mail* and the *Sunday Mail*, Brisbane; the *Mercury*, Hobart; the *West Australian*, Perth; regional dailies throughout Queensland, and the Australian Broadcasting Corporation.

CONTENTS

INTRODUCTION

MOTHER OF THE GUMNUTS

It's hard to tell, hard to say, I don't know if the bush babies found me or I found the little creatures.

May Gibbs interview, 1968

Although they colonised a land rich in native legend and lore, homesick new settlers carried with them to Australia, among other comforts of home, their own creatures of fantasy. All the denizens of British nursery tales—Irish leprechauns, Welsh Kelpies, Scots brownies, and English pixies, fairies and goblins—were standard fare for white Australian children for over a century. Surrounded by a landscape wildly different from the gentle flower- and toadstool-sprinkled meadows of their beautifully illustrated picture books, where elves painted leaves red in autumn and fairies gorgeous in flowing robes and dragonfly wings floated in pastel twilights, it would not have been at all surprising if Australian children had decided that their own environment just wasn't proper fairy country.

When Australian fairy books began to appear, native animals of the gentler sort were seen to mingle with the familiar rabbits, and the prettiest wildflowers clustered with the daisies in dim woods and on grassy hills. Elegant, well-dressed European fairies settled into their adopted home. But the grey-green bush, with its ragged scribbly-bark gums and small, dry flowers, its brown creeks and rough bush tracks, continued to hold its own secrets.

One woman changed all that.

At much the same time as Beatrix Potter and Kenneth Grahame were sharing their observations of the English countryside and giving character to the animals of field and hedgerow, a young artist on the other side of the world was looking at Australian animals and seeing their potential as story characters. But, more importantly, gradually evolving in her mind was a unique response to the Australian bushland that was to result in a rich national mythology.

The artist was May Gibbs, her creation the bush world of the gumnuts Snugglepot and Cuddlepie, their cousins Bib and Bub and a host of other gumnut and other wildflower babies: a world of scribbly writing, koalas, possums, bull ants and beetles, kind old lizards, evil snakes and the horribly wicked, uncouth and cruel Banksia Men. Her unique vision so captured the hearts and imaginations of generations of Australians that today the bush babies—those little plump bare-bottomed figures with their gum-nut hats or ragged-blossom skirts and their wide blue eyes—have become national symbols; gumnut words like 'deadibones' have entered the language; and for decades adults have remembered with a smile as they walked in the bush, the fearful respect with which they once regarded banksia trees. For children and adults alike May Gibbs brought magic as near as the bush was to their doorstep.

She began her career as an illustrator of other people's work, and at first produced the attractive but conventional vision of fairyland with Australian 'props' that was gradually taking the place of purely English scenes.

But slowly a complete Australian bush fairyland started to grow in her imagination and its inhabitants to creep into her illustrations almost unbidden. The forerunners of the gumnuts can be seen in illustrations done in 1913. In the following year a bookmark and several covers featuring wildflower babies as well as gumnuts appeared. There was a series of cards for the armed forces—now valuable collectors' items, but then familiar sights at the front. In the muddy trenches of France and on the sun-dried plains of Palestine, war-weary soldiers opened their Red Cross parcels and welcomed hand-knitted socks, woollen balaclavas and a cheeky message from one of the May Gibbs gumnuts.

We are the gumnut Corp
We're going to the War
(We'll make things hum by gum!)

Then, the books began. *Gum-Nut Babies* and *Gum-Blossom Babies* were the first Australian titles May both wrote and illustrated, and the critical response to them was quite extraordinary:

> *Gum-Nut Babies* and *Gum-Blossom Babies* are two of the quaintest of distinctly Australian booklets that have been put on the market. It is too late in the day to expatiate on the pretty conceit and cleverness of these little studies for their popularity has long since spread over the continent. Miss May Gibbs is an institution of which we are

unreservedly proud, and we want the other side of the world to know about her.

The Bookman, *Sunday Times*, London, 7 October 1917

Miss May Gibbs, the inventor of the 'gumnut baby' further develops her whimsical idea with clever draughtsmanship. These little creatures belong to the same category as the leprechauns of Irish fairy tales. The artist gives a quaint individuality to her little people and, if the world is not getting too materialistic, she may perhaps be laying the foundation of a new Australian folklore.

Evening News, Sydney, 1917

The *Evening News'* forecast proved correct. *Gum-Nut Babies* and *Gum-Blossom Babies* were indeed the foundation of a new folklore, and three more booklets, *Boronia Babies, Flannel Flowers and Other Bush Babies* and *Wattle Babies* followed, to build May Gibbs' achievement. But had she stopped there, with these pretty fancies, beautifully executed paintings accompanied by whimsical and imaginative little snippets of prose, her books would have endured only so far as fashion and patriotism decreed. As has happened with several of her contemporaries, her illustrations would have survived, and her stories been forgotten or reprinted only to satisfy a vogue for nostalgia or 'Australiana'.

But she did not stop there. Between the publication of the first two bush babies booklets and the last three, May Gibbs started writing and illustrating *Tales of Snugglepot and Cuddlepie,* which, together with its sequels *Little Ragged Blossom* and *Little Obelia,* filled out and defined her bushland fantasy world and became the benchmark by which all other Australian children's books are measured. Combined in one volume, *The Complete Adventures of Snugglepot and Cuddlepie* in 1940, the three Snugglepot and Cuddlepie books have never been out of print and have remained Australia's most popular children's classics to this day. They have triumphed over wartime paper restrictions, depression, the competition posed by floods of brightly coloured picture books from overseas and increasing numbers of vigorous new native productions. They continue to flourish in the computer/television/spacetravel/nuclear age as they flourished in the days when a horse and buggy was still the most reliable form of transport.

May Gibbs' work has survived and flourished because she was a true original who knew her audience well. The power of her images has never failed; her vision has never dated. Among the unstinting praise on the release of *Tales of Snugglepot and Cuddlepie* was a piece from the *Sunday Times*, Sydney:

> Snugglepot and Cuddlepie are the quaintest possible creatures and as ingenious in their opportunism as their originator. A book of which children will never tire.

May Gibbs' books have become part of Australia's consciousness because indeed children have never tired of them. They mirror life as children see it: a series of adventures, dangers, happinesses and griefs with no tidy endings or pat solutions. The gumnuts themselves survive perils and misfortunes, meet bad people as well as good. They see unfairness and unhappiness, are terrified by monsters and rescued by kindly strangers. Their world is detailed and busy, and for all its fascinating, amusing bush invention, very similar to the world children know—full of bustling people going about their own affairs while small dramas unfold about them.

No sentimentality intrudes to weaken the effect, or dim the power of the images and impressions. Every glimpse of bush recalls the magical illustrations, so children carry the visions given to them into adulthood, to pass them on to their own children in turn.

Perhaps May Gibbs wrote so well for her chosen audience because, in truth, the child in her never left her. Yet she was in her mid-thirties when the bush babies blossomed under her pen, and to tell her story we must go to the other side of the world, and to the year 1877 . . .

1

THE GIBBS AND ROGERS FAMILIES

'Mrs Gibbs here?'
'Er, yes, er, sir, that's her singing.'
'Powerful voice,' said Dr Stork, cocking his head to listen, momentarily distracted from his mission. 'Right, smooth, round and mellow,' were the words of the music lover.
'Yes, sir,' agreed the bewildered maid.
'Tell her I'm come,' said Dr Stork, balancing his black bag on the hall stand as he hung up his coat and hat. He opened the top of the bag and peered in.
'Warm and snuggled,' he said, 'but a little restless.'
'Yes, sir,' said the maid, who was unable to move her feet so stared into the bag.
'Looks like a frog sir,' she gasped, 'just like her ma.'

This Other Fair(y) Tale, notes for autobiography

May Gibbs was born Cecilia May Gibbs in Cheam Fields, Surrey, on 17 January 1877. For someone who was to immortalise its creatures, both real and imagined, she started life a long way away from the Australian bushland. Her parents, Herbert William Gibbs and Cecilia May Rogers, were quite talented artists, and although neither of them achieved great fame, their talent was sufficient to take each of them to the Slade School of Art in London where they met and fell in love.

Herbert Gibbs came from generations of prosperous county farmers who, in his grandfather's time, had moved from Somerset to Sussex and settled on a large farm in Itchenor, a few kilometres from Chichester. Once the seat of the Duke of Richmond it boasted valuable land and a fine manor house and it was here that Herbert Gibbs' father, William, was born, the youngest of four children and the only son.

The three girls had married well and, having launched them successfully, the Gibbs may have been forgiven for expecting their only son to honour them with a marriage of distinction. It was a bitter blow when the boy announced his intention of marrying the daughter of a struggling farmer who was considered his social inferior. Despite his father's opposition, William Gibbs married Eliza Emery at St Dunstan's in West London, and was thereby disinherited. This is the only known act of rebellion in the early Gibbs family but William displayed a strength of character which was later to distinguish his son, Herbert, and his granddaughter, May.

May Gibbs' maternal grandparents, Nathaniel and Jeanette Rogers, were in marked contrast to the rather staid Gibbs family. They were part of the new free-thinking generation emerging in Victorian England in the latter part of the nineteenth century.

The Georgian house at Gander Green Lane, Cheam Fields, Surrey, seemed to be filled to overflowing by the Rogers family, exuberant in their love for each other and their natural zest for living. Nathaniel, a successful business man, was head of a liberated household and both he and Jeanette, who had been given a full schooling in France by her parents, ensured that the girls received as complete an education as the boys, something considered radical in most circles at that time. It was a household which respected art in all its forms. Jeanette was an accomplished poet with several published volumes and all the girls had fine singing voices, so that musical evenings were a regular and greatly enjoyed part of their week.

Despite the modern approach to education, the girls followed the tradition of the period with early marriages and most were engaged in their teens. Only the youngest, Cecie, had shown no interest in gentlemen callers, being quite immersed in piano lessons, singing and her course at the Slade School of Art. This entailed travelling to London by train each day and it was while commuting that Cecie met the young Herbert Gibbs.

Herbert was a rather serious young man, tall and handsome, but made self-conscious by an affliction in one of his eyes. When fifteen years of age, he had 'poked his head from behind a tree at the wrong moment', and a wayward dart pierced his left eye. Gradually he lost the sight of it. The injury caused strain and frequent headaches and Herbert was forced to leave school at an early age. His father arranged a tutor for him, Edward Coke, a local curate who was an extremely talented man and an Oxford chum of lyricist W. S. Gilbert. Consequently, Herbert's education was thorough and included the arts.

He was also a competent sailor, he and his brother George being virtually raised on the southern waters of England. Perhaps like most young men of the time, discontented with the old ways and the lack of opportunity, they talked of sailing across the seas for a new life in the vastly growing empire. These plans were shelved (although only temporarily as it happened) when Herbert Gibbs met Cecie Rogers on the train to London.

Despite certain misgivings—he was only twenty, two years younger than Cecie, and employed as a clerk at the GPO—Cecie's parents were enchanted with Herbert. He was well versed in the social graces, was kind and gentle and obviously captivated by Cecie's charm and vitality. He, in turn, warmed to the joyful atmosphere of the Rogers household.

It might be supposed that William and Eliza Gibbs would hardly be in a position to frown on the prospect of Cecie Rogers as a daughter-in-law but, despite the fact that they had defied William's parents with their own marriage, they objected to the Rogers being Plymouth Brethren, therefore 'Chapel', while the Gibbs were 'Church'. This was a consideration of little import to the participating couple, who announced their intention of marrying. The Gibbs were finally won over by Cecie and gave their blessing.

Following their marriage, Herbert was absorbed into the Rogers family. He and Cecie were constant visitors at Gander Green Lane and it was during one of their visits there that May was born. She was their second child. Their first, Bertie, had been born eighteen months earlier. In accordance with the custom of the day, the first son was named after the father and the first daughter after the mother, Cecilia May. The children were known as Bertie and Mamie.

The first four years of May's life, she always claimed to remember in vivid detail. Indeed some of the memories she later recorded in preparation for an autobiography reveal the keen observation of character that is an important part of her writing.

> 'Bon Pa' my maternal Grandfather I remember by the way he buttered his toast at the table.
>
> Very quickly he spread the butter on and off several times.
>
> I would stand beside the huge rounded table legs, mouth wide as a baby bird—getting little tit-bits from the big hand above the table edge.

> My maternal Grandmother 'Bon Ma'. I remember a soft plump smiling face, loving dark eyes looking at me, my two fat hands one on each side of her cheeks. The big pillow behind her head.
>
> First time left alone was in a big place, below ground, my mother dressed for going out, hat, muffs, cloak and gloves, kissed me and hurried away closing the door—she was gone. I opened my mouth and roared—I was left behind—everything turned black—couldn't see—my mother gone. Suddenly someone's arms were around me, 'Poor little darling, you shall come with us.'
>
> Driving behind a big, big horse between my aunt and uncle, I sat well wrapped and happy as we spanked along hedges and trees and fields flying past.
>
> 'Quite comfy?' said my aunt, tucking me more firmly into the rug.
>
> First annoyance, the aunt who chased me round and round the table with a doll nearly as big as me. I was frightened, didn't like her. Same aunt put gooseberry leaves in back of my dress, pulled them out and said, 'Oh! See what's growing out of you, because you eat green gooseberries.'
>
> First Embarrassment. The surprise picture for my mother—Aunt E takes the children to the photographer, just as they are leaving little girl wets her drawers, a much too large pair of her cousin's is quickly popped on. The picture is shocking and always brought out by brother to show, when sister has visitors.

She was hopelessly spoilt by grandparents and aunts and uncles, whose numbers appeared to be endless. But it was at her grandmother's knee she learned poetry, and Jeanette's light-hearted creations, especially her sonnets to her grandchildren, were, undoubtedly, the great influence on the later writing of her granddaughter.

The Gibbs had been married six years when Herbert's failing eyesight forced him to consider George's often voiced urgings about the new land. The office where he worked in St Mark's Road was badly lit and the work tedious. With the eye strain the headaches returned and Herbert was advised to seek alternative employment.

The Gibbs had been farmers for generations, as George kept reminding him, and large stretches of land were being offered throughout South Australia as the Government wooed free settlers from the homeland. Distant relatives had already answered the call and had taken up land near Adelaide.

It was mid-winter in England when a letter arrived from a cousin, Captain Teasdel, lauding the Australian climate, the constant blue skies and warm sunshine. The captain also graphically described the 'good grazing land stretching for miles about Franklin Harbour, South Australia'. Herbert discussed the prospect with Cecie whose adventurous spirit immediately responded to the call of a new life. Neither Herbert nor George was aware of any discrepancy between the lifestyle of the English farmer and the Australian settler. They were confident that they would succeed.

Finally, after checking finances, passages were booked and Herbert Gibbs and family, plus brother George, were ready to sail for Australia.

There was, however, to be a last minute change of plan!

A week before departure, as her parents bustled with their packing, young May was hardly noticed with her persistent sneezing. The sneezing developed into a racking cough, accompanied by a running nose and feverish brow and soon the child was running a high temperature. The proposed journey was almost forgotten as, for three days, Herbert and Cecie waited anxiously for the crisis. When it came, it was followed by a mass of tell-tale spots—measles.

The common measles in the nineteenth century was a disease which killed a great number of its victims, as the family bibles of the day so sadly testify. It seemed that it was also to put an end to the Gibbs' travel plans as no passenger would be allowed to sail with a known infectious disease. In her positive fashion, Cecie declared that the brothers should make the journey as scheduled and she and the children would follow when May was able to travel.

Reluctantly, Herbert agreed and he and George sailed for Australia.

2

FAILURE AT FRANKLIN

A big square tank — water had to be carted from four miles away — surrounded by birds fighting for a drink. A hot dry red place with not a drop of moisture anywhere.

This Other Fair(y) Tale,
notes for autobiography

The Gibbs brothers landed at Port Adelaide from the Orient steamer *Chimborago,* on 1 June 1881. Urged by his sons Herbert later wrote an account of their first weeks in Australia. He recorded that they found the port town lacking in welcome and inhabited by larrikins whose dialects originated in all corners of the British Isles; an ugly town, the unpaved streets sending up dust in the unfamiliar heat, which lingered into the night when the population were nearly devoured by mosquitoes.

The following day the brothers went to the Lands Office in Adelaide where they were advised of the location of the land which had been selected for them by Captain Teasdel. They paid what was necessary to secure about 1220 hectares and the next day they sailed to Wallaroo on Spencer Gulf, taking with them only what they could carry. The rest of their luggage was to follow by small ketch in a few weeks.

On reaching Wallaroo they engaged a fisherman and his son to take them across the 72 kilometres to Franklin Harbour and then 10 kilometres up the harbour. In order to get there by sunset, they set off at midnight but the wind fell to nearly a calm and it was 10 p.m. before they reached their destination. There being no jetty they were deposited some 180 metres from the shore. By the light of the moon, they stripped and, with their kit and clothing on their heads, walked through mud, rocks and mangroves to reach it.

One can imagine the utter despair which overtook the brothers that first night at Franklin Harbour. Cold, damp, threatened by a large assortment of strange crawling insects, Herbert must have acknowledged, if only to himself, that he had made a mistake. It was a far cry from the warmth of Gander Green Lane.

The clean, sunny morning restored some of their good humour. Plenty of water from the previous day's rain could be found in some old bullock wagon tracks and they were able to make tea and have a fairly good breakfast.

There were, of course, no cleared roads in the area and the directions they had been given for Teasdel's farm were very sketchy. They knew it was approximately 10 kilometres in a westerly direction, so they set off along the best defined track.

About 5 kilometres on they came to a store, a rough building where a young merchant was offering supplies to the settlers, including boots, moleskin trousers, hats and shirts. He was able to direct them on the further 5 kilometres to Captain Teasdel's station. The captain's glowing reports to his relatives back in England had depicted a far more comfortable scene than any they had encountered since reaching Franklin Harbour or were experiencing now as they pushed their way through the high mallee scrub. When they finally arrived at the 'farm', their disillusionment was complete.

They saw a rough camp, a house with tin walls and a hessian roof, a tin shed which the captain called 'the store', the area surrounded by a bush fence—posts set up in pairs with the space filled with mallee tops. The only redeeming feature of the area appeared to be the good supply of water, and the flock of about 200 sheep Teasdel was running appeared to be in healthy condition.

What prompted Captain Teasdel to send the fanciful reports to his relatives back home? Loneliness and a desire to ensure others would join him, embarrassment because he had been duped into settling on worthless land or a cruel streak which wanted to see others suffer?

Over the months to follow, the Gibbs brothers were to decide it was the last. Without their own gear, the men were unable to start work on their land, so they came to an agreement with Teasdel to work for him for their 'tucker' until their supplies arrived. The captain made sure they earned their keep and Herbert and George settled down to battle with the strange elements of the new country and its harsh way of life.

While Herbert battled, 20,000 kilometres away Cecie discovered she was again pregnant. Despite horrendous tales of ships disappearing in the Indian Ocean and with no assurance that her husband had even reached his destination, she announced that she was leaving for Australia immediately.

The decision naturally brought a chorus of protests from her family. Apart from their genuine concern about the dangers inherent in such a trip, Nathaniel and Jeanette had enjoyed having their grandchildren for this additional period and had succeeded in utterly spoiling four-year-old May. In the pampered environs of her measles convalescence, she spent a great deal of time in the sitting room, tucked up in an enormous chair while everyone paid court. It was always Bertie's job—Captain Bertie she called him—to organise the games around her. They inevitably centred on the sailing ship which Captain Bertie would fashion from the furniture and in which May would feature as a princess, slave or singer.

Protests, counselling, pleading, all were to no avail for Cecie had a streak of stubbornness—a trait she would bequeath to her daughter and which would be the basis for many of their arguments in later years. With her two children and a third pregnancy quite well advanced, Cecie left in July 1881 for the three-month journey to Australia on the sailing ship *Hesperus*.

Fortunately, she and the children proved to be good sailors and both Bertie and May had an insatiable curiosity about everything on the ship. They were befriended by one of the sailors, Tom McKiney, who introduced them to life at sea so that they knew every section of the three-masted barque. From Tom, May also learned some of the sea shanties of the day, which caused some embarrassment when she insisted on entertaining the passengers in the evenings. She was obviously a precocious child, and she knew it.

> I was four years old and everywhere I was a star performer and took it quite seriously.

Cecie continued to walk briskly on deck, confident that the vessel would reach Adelaide well before her baby was due. Unfortunately, the elements had scant respect for the schedule of pregnancy. After rounding the Cape of Good Hope and sailing with the prevailing westerlies out of the Atlantic, the *Hesperus* enjoyed two weeks' propulsion by the Roaring Forties, only to be left becalmed as the mighty wind dropped. For two weeks the large barque lay motionless on a glassy sea. The heat became unbearable and the passengers distressed and irritable.

A distraction arranged by the captain was a dip in the ocean. One of the huge sails was lowered over the side to form an enclosure and the men and boys were able to dive from the side of the ship into the makeshift pool. Bertie was able to join in the fun and May was loud in her protest against the rules that limited the fun to the men and boys.

By this time, it was obvious to everyone on board that Cecie was pregnant and every day's delay made it more likely that the baby would be born at sea. With some agitation, Cecie would peer out to sea, searching for the white horses which should appear on the horizon, announcing the arrival of the wind. As one still day followed another, she became reconciled to the fact that the arrival of the baby would be announced first.

They arrived together. As the white horses appeared in the distance and the sails began to flap gently, Cecie went into labour and Ivan, the 'Wreck of the *Hesperus*' as he was later to describe himself, joined the family of adventurers. Three weeks later, in November 1881, the *Hesperus* made port in Australia.

Port Adelaide was the same dirty, dusty town that Herbert Gibbs had found and it must have been with some trepidation that Cecie said goodbye to the *Hesperus* and the months of shipboard companionship.

From the moment she decided to leave England, Cecie had obviously experienced no doubt about her ability to cope with any situation. Ashore in the unaccustomed heat, with two small children in tow and one in arms, no friendly face offering greeting and no idea of her husband's whereabouts, surely even Cecie's indomitable spirit would have faltered? But she had to find her husband so, like Herbert, she made her way to the Lands Department, carrying a large suitcase, and with baby Ivan on one arm. Bertie and May kept close, each struggling with bundles far too large for them.

Once she'd located Herbert, Cecie was obviously anxious to join him but was then informed that the small vessel which made the trip to Franklin Harbour every three months was not due to leave for another month. Armed with a letter of introduction to distant relatives, Cecie and her small party were directed from one address to another until they finally found a home where they were made welcome while they waited for transport.

Finally the small coaster was ready to leave, and they were off to sea again. This trip was in marked contrast to the voyage on the *Hesperus*, but they enjoyed travelling around the South Australian inlets, with their profusion of unusual bird life. As the boat nosed in among the mangroves and marshes to collect a passenger or deliver stores to lonely outposts, flocks of wild water birds would rise into the sky.

Finally they were at Franklin Harbour, only to face a rowing-boat ride through marshes and a piggy-back to firm ground where a sorry-looking horse and cart met the boat to pick up supplies and passengers. After hours of uncomfortable jolting over the makeshift road, they arrived at a newly cleared area on which stood a two-room slab hut—the Gibbs homestead.

If Herbert Gibbs' first view of his Franklin accommodation produced disappointment and despair, one can imagine the misery with which the young lady from Gander Green Lane surveyed the shack that was to be home for her and her three small children. But Cecie's resilience did not desert her, and by the time Herbert and George returned from their chores, she had suppressed her horror and was ready to welcome the husband she had not seen for many months.

When they emerged from the bush, George was carrying a wild turkey which he had just shot while Herbert had a bag of root vegetables and a small spray of sturdy Australian wildflowers. It was an exciting and loving reunion in the midst of which May recalls taking possession of the bouquet—her introduction to the flowers which were later to inspire her.

The transformation of the brothers must have been a shock to Cecie. Both had lost weight and the long arduous hours in the sun had aged them. It took Cecie only a matter of weeks to recognise the hopelessness of the settlement at Franklin Harbour. Her neighbours, most of whom were living in tents and some of whom had been there for four and five years, were still trying to understand the harsh land. One young woman who had come from a similar background to her own, was living nearby in a tent and had been crying almost continually since her arrival, unable to cope with the shock of the contrast of conditions. Cecie herself was struggling with a new lifestyle which had her not only housekeeping for two grown men but taking care of three small children. Gone were the halcyon days of Cheam Fields where servants took care of the menial tasks and a regiment of grandparents and aunts fought to spoil the children.

One of the factors which had induced Herbert to stay in the area was the good supply of water but a hot dry Australian summer had soon swallowed up that attraction and they were now in the midst of a drought.

Water became precious and had to be carted from 2 kilometres away. The Gibbs' water supply in a tank near the hut was gradually invaded by Australian wildlife driven in from the surrounding dry country as their waterholes disappeared. Birds in a riot of coloured plumage, a wide variety of lizards, various brilliant beetles and insects of all sorts—all were fascinating. The little English girl would sit near the tank enticing them with saucers of water. There being no one else to play with, these creatures became her friends. Bertie was considered big enough to help his father and uncle with the chores—and her mother was most often too busy to be company. May being too small to help and too big to be helped, was thus left a great deal to herself. It was a strange kindergarten for a little four-year-old girl, its harshness far removed from the soft, warm world of 'Bon Ma', but to a budding artist whose skills must include the powers of observation it was a great schoolroom.

The lack of water demanded further sacrifices. Baby Ivan had to be bathed in a breakfast cup of water each day and when there was no spare water for the other children's ablutions, Cecie chopped off May's mass of auburn curls which had become caked with dust, and both mother and daughter cried.

Apart from her own abhorrence of the conditions, Cecie recognised Herbert's spirit was breaking under the hopelessness of their situation and convinced him to cut his losses and return to Adelaide for a new start. Eventually it was agreed that she and the children should depart on the next three-monthly boat while Herbert and George stayed only to dispose of the property. So three months after their arrival, Cecie and her brood returned to Adelaide.

Herbert watched his family loaded into the little coastal boat, then made his way back to the slab hut. That night he wrote in his diary in large letters, 'Failure at Franklin'.

Cecie found an old cottage for rent in Norwood, an outer suburb of Adelaide. It was not elaborate but it was surrounded by a rambling garden with almond trees and a picturesque well. Once she had furnished it with her possessions from England, until then unpacked, she had a neatly comfortable home waiting for Herbert when he arrived three months later.

After a short holiday, George took on the management of a pastoral property at St Auburns, a few kilometres from Adelaide, while Herbert looked for employment. With the heavy flow of hopeful migrants and unsuccessful farmers into the city, unemployment was high but the Lands Department was seeking experienced draftsmen and Herbert found himself once more behind a drafting board.

The children loved their home in Norwood, particularly the garden, which not only supported them with vegetables but provided the beauty of flowers. Bertie was now going to school but, in accordance with the custom of the day, May received her education at home. In this, she was indeed fortunate because both Herbert and Cecie had been excellent students and they were also good teachers. In fact Cecie had, for a short time, followed a teaching career and had the natural enthusiasm of someone anxious to impart knowledge. Cecie instructed May during the day and, in the evenings, her father would read with her. He was particularly gratified by her interest in art and would take her walking in the bush where together they would sketch a landscape and wildlife new to them. At a very early age May demonstrated a talent for sketching by copying a book of Caldecott drawings, and the finely detailed drawings proved to be excellent training for the illustrations of the future.

> My parents were wonderful. They were so happy together. I never remember them falling out, and they were awfully good to us children. I was never smacked. Of course, I suppose I was spoilt. And I loved drawing, so my father started me right off, because he was a clever artist.

Sunday afternoons were for resting on the grass near the well when Cecie would read from Dickens or the papers from 'home'. In two years they had brought a little corner of Surrey to Adelaide and the 'Failure at Franklin' became a dim memory.

On the voyage to Australia the Gibbs brothers had become friendly with two other migrants, a Dr Henry Harvey and a Mr John Young. Henry Harvey had been on his way to Western Australia when his wife had contracted a serious illness and he was delayed in Adelaide. John Young had taken up land in Franklin Harbour with the same pitiful results as the Gibbs.

The four men had remained in touch and, as an investment, together bought a small farm in Auburn in South Australia. In addition, they had augmented their funds by investing in mining shares and other small pieces of real estate. But there was still the old dream of owning a 'property', a big property where they could use the skills so painfully acquired at Franklin Harbour. When the Stirling Estate in Western Australia was advertised, it caught their attention.

> This area of 12,800 acres was selected by Governor Stirling in 1829 and combines hills and flat. It has a good rainfall and rich soil. The homestead was originally built by the Governor and considerably extended by J. Thompson Logue, who built the brick house from bricks made on the property.

Harvey and Young were interested in the proposition as an investment so, with adequate support to ensure it was not under-capitalised, the Gibbs brothers were optimistic.

And so the Harvey, Young and Gibbs Pastoral Company was born and the 5200 hectares of the Stirling Estate became 'The Harvey'. They also leased 8090 hectares of grazing land at Collie so they had their big property. In August 1885 Herbert Gibbs resigned from the South Australian Lands Department and prepared for the new venture.

Again, the men were to go ahead but this time Bertie accompanied them, with Cecie, Ivan and May following some months later. During the 2400-kilometre sea voyage to Western Australia May assumed the instructional role Bertie had had on their first voyage, directing Ivan with an authority which soon irked him.

The family arrived at Bunbury in the spring, transferred from the ship to a coach and headed north along the Perth road.

3
THE HARVEY

The Harvey River Homestead— there two years, wonderful years. The two happiest years of my life.

This Other Fair(y) Tale,
notes for autobiography

If the family had had qualms, perhaps expecting another pioneering stint, they would have been happy to find that the area in which their new home was situated was considered quite civilised.

The district, about 58,300 hectares square, lay on the foothills and coastal plain between the Darling Range and the Indian Ocean and looked 48 kilometres south to Bunbury and 138 kilometres north to Perth.

Its settlers came from the English and Anglo-Irish middle class and skilled artisan class and were literate and proud of their education. They were Church of England and preserved their religion in spite of the absence of clergy, each settler being quite familiar with the ritual of service of the church. They were modern folk who called in the doctor and did not depend on folk remedies as did many of their contemporaries.

Most of the homesteads in the area were large—generally a main house surrounded by two or three small cottages for the workmen. The owner spent most of his time riding out on the property, while his wife supervised family, kitchen, dairy and garden. As the family grew, it was possible to use their own labour instead of outsiders. There were tasks for all according to age, beginning with scaring birds, and going on to reaping corn, herding sheep and milking cows. At the house there was milk to be skimmed, butter to be churned and cheese to be set down, soap and candles to be made, bacon to be cured and meat to be corned. There were always men working around the homestead, building sheds and new rooms, shingle splitting, threshing and winnowing wheat, pruning vines and perhaps making wine. It was a pioneering area of young farmers and here the Gibbs were to make another start.

The old convict-built homestead on The Harvey was roomy. It boasted a drawing room, dining room, several bedrooms and an office for the manager, Herbert Gibbs. Under a separate roof, close to the main building, were the kitchen, pantry and another bedroom. Some distance up a pathway edged with fruit trees were the men's quarters, workshops and stables.

When the family arrived at the property, the orchard trees were laden with oranges and grouped around the house was a selection of trees bearing other fruits: apples, peaches, figs, apricots, plums.

To one side of The Harvey homestead a grassy edge ran down about a metre to the bank of the Harvey River and the steep banks on the far side were covered with maidenhair fern, which harboured snakes and lizards. Above the jungle of ferns were huge rocks and boulders and the children climbed to the top of them to view the Indian Ocean which could be seen some 20 kilometres off.

In the winter the river ran with a full swift current. During the summer it dwindled to occasional deep pools, linked by the merest trickle. They had tubs for boats.

> A big one for my brother, a lesser one for me and a little one for Ivan, who was only four. We would paddle around and shore them on the white sandy beach.

Along with her brothers, May learned to swim in the deep holes of the river and also about its denizens: koonacks (freshwater prawns), little coloured fish, frogs under logs, and dozens of creatures which inhabited the moss-covered rocks, white sands, muddy banks and fallen trees along the ever-changing landscape of the stream.

While the children explored their new paradise and Cecie settled into her kitchen, Herbert and George worked the property with the help of a group of Aborigines. It was hard work and there was no time for hobbies, so few sketches depicting this period appear in Herbert's portfolio.

But more practical accomplishments were recorded with pride.

> Father learned to make beautiful butter and we children helped turning the handle of the churn. In the same room big preserve jars stood on a shelf so high that red juice ran down our arms and the stain told the tale of adventurous fingers.
>
> The homestead had an old brick oven in the kitchen and mother learned to make good bread. One of the tasks we children enjoyed was using the long spade putting in and taking out the loaves.

The kitchen also enticed unwanted guests—guests whom few pioneers wished to entertain and once entertained, rarely forgot.

> One day the heat of the oven attracted a large black snake to the kitchen. I reached up for a plate on the shelf and saw its long body worming slowly up between the rough wooden slabs. I stared in wonderment and it slithered away quickly before I could raise the alarm.

May had never realised the black snake was a frequent visitor until her father pointed out the indentations on the freshly swept earthen path to the house. Inspections of the path revealed that May had enchanted the snake with her daily practice session of scales and exercises. Before a practice session the path was swept and after the session there was the evidence of snake tracks, right up to the French windows beside the piano. No one ever caught the music lover.

There was no school within riding distance of the homestead and in the beginning the task of educating the children fell to Cecie, who was relieved when a tutor started to make the rounds of the farms and stations and included The Harvey homestead in this circuit. But her pleasure was short-lived. Dicka Dean, the tutor, was not highly qualified for the task nor had he much experience. The first few visits proved a mild success with Bertie and May showing necessary respect and making an attempt at learning but baby Ivan soon overcame his awe and became quite disruptive. Due no doubt to his inexperience and lack of confidence, the tutor complained to their mother not of their behaviour but of their lack of ability, a criticism which was not received kindly. Disobedient, maybe, but her children lacking in ability? Cecie dismissed him and the children celebrated his departure. But Cecie was determined they should learn and resumed the responsibility herself.

Dividing the pupils into separate rooms, she set them tasks at their individual levels and endeavoured to give them a comprehensive education, though a bias towards the arts was always evident in Cecie's teaching.

The children all tended to view their English history books with some distaste and found writing and arithmetic even more laborious. However, all were endured because, once over, Cecie took out her favourite children's books. With her fine speaking voice, she brought the pages of *Brer Rabbit, Alice Through the*

Looking Glass, Little Women, and the English *Boy's Own Annual* alive for Bertie, May and Ivan. May enjoyed these sessions immensely and when it came her turn to read, would carefully imitate her mother's phraseology and delivery. This tuition was the basis for May's beautifully modulated voice, which was to become her most commanding feature.

Music appreciation was a natural part of their curriculum and musical evenings became important social occasions. Two or three days' notice were given and the neighbours from nearby stations would gather at one residence for the entertainment. Everyone was expected to participate. Eight-year-old May had announced to her family her intention of becoming a famous actress and suffered no shy reticence on such occasions. She never had to be coerced into performing.

Sundays were the highlight of the week and were days of rest and relaxation. Thompson Logue, a neighbouring farmer, assumed the Sunday role of lay-preacher and sometimes arrived at the station to give a service. It was a serious business. The family and staff gathered in the largest room in the homestead and dutifully listened to Thompson Logue's ponderous reading of the lesson. It was generally an attentive gathering, though May was more impressed with her father's ability to stop the entrance of the homestead's dogs into the room with a slight motion of his hand than with the content of the preaching. For the children the service became real entertainment when the preacher was accompanied by his son. Archibald Logue was a little less reverent than the rest of the congregation. At regular intervals he piped up, 'Read on a little faster, Daddy, and have done with it.' Thompson would pause, inspect the boy over his reading glasses and, in his most studied parsonic voice, command, 'Be quiet, Archie!' This interchange invariably enlivened the service and brought giggles and squirms from the Gibbs children. 'Be quiet, Archie!' became a treasured family saying.

Also on Sundays, Cecie permitted the children to go off alone on a picnic. It gave them a sense of adventure to spend a day in the bush, out of range of parental control. May recalled vivid memories of these outings. Led by Captain Bertie, carrying his gun and knapsack packed with victuals, the three adventurers would balance across the fallen log bridging the stream, clamber up through the ferns on the side of the bank, turn to wave farewell to

Cecie seated on the veranda of the homestead and then disappear from view.

> Bertie was allowed to take his gun. For about two miles we examined the bush for nests, strange creatures, new flowers, and everything was of intense interest. We made a hut with branches and roofed it with thatch made of brittle green stems off the top of grass trees. Bertie proved his marksmanship by bringing a parrot to earth with a single shot, which he plucked, cleaned and cooked and we had for lunch.

In later years, May Gibbs would have abhorred the death of the parrot, but in 1886 it was purely part of a day of adventure.

When she was about nine years old May's boundaries were widened unexpectedly. An agent, who periodically visited the homestead, arrived one day mounted on a small brown pony. May fell in love with the pony and pleaded with her father to buy it for her. Herbert seemed unmoved by her request but when the agent came again, he was riding another horse and leading the pony, which was presented to May.

'Brownie' made it possible for May to escape the confines of the homestead and become an explorer. She was able to visit the stations and farm within riding distance, but more importantly it gave her the chance to study the Australian bush. The flowers in the surrounding scrub enchanted her. Spider orchids, white with red tongues, standing about 60 centimetres tall, bachelor buttons pushing through the green foliage, papery everlastings, brown boronia scenting the countryside. There was always something in bloom no matter what the time of year.

A boundary of her wanderings was the bridge which led to the main road. Gentle grassy slopes ran down to the water's edge and one side was rather swampy with white shaggy-stemmed paperbark trees.

Along the main road, where she could catch a glimpse of the Cobb and Co. coach pounding up to Perth, the spreads of small white everlasting daisy provided bunches of tiny flowers to trim the large shady hat which Cecie insisted be worn on all adventures.

May became quite an identity in the district, the red-haired Gibbs girl on her pony.

> Visited a farm some miles away. Children all peeped at me from behind corners of the house and windows, about 10 of them. If I

> approached them they scattered away like rabbits. The eldest was twelve, but a little old woman.

And Brownie bridged the distance between new-found friends.

> Riding two miles to the next station home, to see the Adams boys, milking the wild bees in a certain tree and the notes we left one another in the hollow burnt out log, each travelling halfway to get letters.

Like most ponies, Brownie tested the mettle of his new owner.

> Brownie stopped at the turn-off to where the cows grazed during the day. I went home in tears and Mother said 'Are you going to let the pony beat you?' Back I went. Coming to the turn-off, I whipped him up but he stops, so I get off and lead him past.

Large social occasions were few but a most happy event was the marriage of Uncle George and Miss Ellen Holden of South Australia on the last day of 1885. George had acquired a separate piece of land, and with the help of Herbert, who had become a proficient bush carpenter, set about building a home for his new bride. In later years, it was a home where May was to spend many happy days, her refuge from the city of Perth.

There was sorrow also when the child Cecie had been carrying for months was stillborn and its little body was buried at The Harvey station.

Then too the business side of 'The Harvey Estate' was anything but happy. The Gibbs brothers were in constant correspondence with their partners, Harvey and Young, and kept them informed of the various farming problems they were experiencing. Henry Harvey's answer to any difficulty was more supplies, so horses, stock and equipment would arrive, creating a fresh problem as there was nowhere to house the new possessions. The men, torn between building and tending the stock, gradually realised they were fighting a losing battle. John Young decided to sell his share to a Dr Hayward, a colleague of Harvey, and the firm became 'Harvey, Hayward and Gibbs'. It was hoped a change of name would mean a change of luck.

However, in 1887, when Henry Harvey arrived in his usual cheerful manner and the partners went over the property and the books, it was obvious that changes had to be made as there now seemed little hope of running the station at a profit. Harvey felt he would try managing the property for a while and his partner offered to buy out the Gibbs brothers, so the firm became Harvey and Hayward.

George Gibbs decided to stay in his newly built home, while Herbert decided to try his luck in Perth. (The Harvey property eventually did become productive, but it was some thirty years later, when the Harvey Irrigation Works was established.)

May was ten years of age when she had to leave The Harvey and the sorrow she felt as a child and the tears she shed remained vivid in her memory. It was her first experience of sorrow. She diligently bade farewell to each of her bush friends, humans and animals. Bade farewell to the playing hideouts and special retreats, the favourite plants and bushes that had become so much a part of her world.

There were promises that the family would return to the area but she felt little confidence that this would eventuate. From her memory, the family regularly tore up roots and then went on lengthy journeys never to return.

May described her time at The Harvey as the 'happiest in my life' and her recollections were filled with its many pleasures. But in recalling these and her adventures she also remembered one obviously jarring incident which took place when the three children had been left at home alone while their parents visited neighbours.

She and Ivan were racing each other and May, victorious, turned to jeer at her opponent before ducking into a shed. Triumph turned to terror as she was grabbed by 'gnarled hands' and held tight. It was old Isaac, an itinerant carpenter who was at that time employed on the property. Whether or not he intended harm to his small captive is not known but May never forgot her fear of 'the bearded face' with 'strange wild eyes'. She remembered, too, extricating herself, picking up a knife lying on a nearby shelf, and threatening her assailant before fleeing the building. And then Bertie running to the rescue, challenging Isaac 'to come out and fight like a man'.

Frightening stuff for an eight-year-old, probably the stuff of nightmares and just possibly as well the germ of an idea. Banksia trees grow throughout much of Australia's coastal zone but it was a banksia tree on The Harvey from which the Big Bad Banksia Men, with their bearded faces and their strange wild eyes, sprang.

4
THE FAMILY IN PERTH

We arrived in Perth and drove into a sort of circular place, then stopped. We walked down the street. If there were one or two people walking in the street it was quite an excitement in Perth.

May Gibbs, interview

Perth of the 1880s was a small town growing on the edge of the River Swan and fed by its port, Fremantle, which straddled the opening of a picturesque inlet on the Western Australian coast. Most of the ocean-going vessels called at Bunbury and Albany in the south, so Perth–Fremantle was not yet the axis of Western Australia.

The majority of the population was English or of English descent, the balance made up of Scots, Irish, Welsh and a small number of representatives from most of the European countries, Asia and North America. Waves of migrants moved into and out of Perth–Fremantle, seeking land and mining opportunities just as their fellow countrymen were doing in the other large Australian cities. However, the inhabitants of Perth felt isolated from the other Australian colonies. It was, after all, some 6500 kilometres closer to Europe than Sydney and Melbourne, and consequently its citizens remained much closer to Mother England than did 'tothersiders'—those of the eastern cities. Western Australian society displayed a reluctance to discard the ways of 'the old country' and its members quickly established a class system based on the society rules they had always known. Certainly money helped to bridge the gap, if one were lacking in social standing, and so did a talent in the arts, which was later to give the Gibbs their entrée.

Still clinging to the dream of a property, no matter how small, Herbert Gibbs took four hectares of land at Butler's Swamp, now the suburb of Claremont, which lies halfway between Perth and Fremantle. May's impressions of it were recorded in notes for her autobiography.

> The Swamp was near the point and there were thousands of mossies (mosquito) and millions of frogs. They began low and gradually

> rose to a note about four notes higher. I often walked down at dusk to hear them. Wonder what sort of frogs they were ... never saw one!

At Claremont, the Gibbs family lived near rather than in the city and, once again, it was almost a country life. Herbert re-roofed the red cottage, cultivated the garden and the dozens of fig trees which surrounded the house. Once again they were near the water which satisfied Herbert's love of the sea. He built a sail boat, *The Gadfly*, in which he would pack all the family and sail down river towards Fremantle. As a result of the excursions in *The Gadfly*, May became a competent sailor and, many years later, was proud of the authenticity of her kurrajong boats—the leaf sails and twig masts, tillers and oars were all based on her practical experience.

They were lazy, fun-filled excursions, generally disorganised, and punctuated by the sight of a picturesque cove, when *The Gadfly* would drop anchor and disgorge tents, chairs, umbrellas, food and children for a picnic lunch ashore.

> My father and mother were such pals. You'd see him sitting on his three-cornered stool in front of an easel with a big board on it, mother sitting beside him, in a more comfortable chair, reading an interesting book ... so I used to come around and perch somewhere.

During this period, Herbert produced a number of satirical cartoons reflecting the social and political scene in Perth and, influenced by these, May produced her own comical observation of members of the household. Herbert nurtured his daughter's talent, recognising that, even at this early age, she had an acute sense of the ridiculous, which is a cartoonist's basic talent. Both were rewarded some years later in 1889 when a drawing of May's illustrating children preparing for Christmas appeared in the Christmas edition of the *W.A. Bulletin*—her first published work.

The Gibbs were gaining a reputation in Perth art circles.* With Bernard Woodward, Director of the Western Australian Museum, G. Temple Pool, the Government Architect, and H. G. Prinsep, Secretary for Mines, they were involved in the establishment in 1890 of a society to encourage the development of young artists' work called the Wilgie Club—'wilgie' being a native name for

* Herbert Gibbs became recognised for his own artistic talent and is represented in the Art Gallery of Western Australia as well as in many private collections.

May as a young girl. The original is executed in oils on wood and was painted by her father, 'H. G.', in 1889.

coloured clay. Aspiring artists submitted their work to them for criticism and help, and, at thirteen, May was in the midst of this and found herself sketching with increasing enthusiasm. Her ability to record events made any occasion an excuse for an imaginative card. Among her drawings for conventional English-style cards to send greetings for Christmas 1890, is an Australian Christmas greeting and it is interesting to note that this is the first record of a May Gibbs drawing of naked children in the bush.

The sadness following the news from England of the death of Jeanette Rogers—their beloved 'Bon Ma'—was softened both by the discovery that Cecie was to have another child and by the arrival in Perth of her eldest brother, Ishmael Rogers, his wife and eight daughters.

Needless to say, the arrival of this large family of close relatives caused quite a diversion. The ship carrying the main part of their household goods had gone down off the coast of Africa but the Rogers accepted the blow philosophically and thanked providence that none of their family was on board. A strong and determined couple, they immediately settled into Perth, Mrs

Rogers establishing a select private school and Ishmael practising as an accountant-stockbroker. He was later to become a foundation member of the Perth Stock Exchange. May's description of Uncle Ishmael Rogers is as revealing as one of her caricatures.

> A proper shape for a Pickwick. Small, fair, blue eyes, round body like a ball. Round fat face, small flat nose and a hearty-chuckling man with a huge appetite.

The companionship of a group of cousins was a new experience for May and when a visit from the 'Rogers girls' was promised, she would be watching up the Perth road for the first glimpse of them riding down on their hired horses. They talked to May of English scenes she 'thought' she could remember and she introduced them to the Australian bush, surprising herself with her own knowledge and consequently acquiring a modicum of self-confidence much needed with her polished English cousins. Herbert noticed the change in his daughter after her cousins' visit. She became a more private person and he would notice her imitating their movements, gestures and accents.

It was undoubtedly the arrival of the Rogers family in their midst which prompted Herbert to take stock of his situation at Claremont. At best he was only eking out an existence with his art tuition, augmented by the sale of figs from the orchard. Certainly they were almost self-sufficient on the farm, the vegetable garden and the dairy supplying most of their needs, but he was suddenly acutely aware of his other obligations to his children, who now needed higher forms of education. It was back to a permanent desk job for Herbert and, in 1889, he joined the Lands Department of Western Australia where he was to spend the rest of his working life.

The city job made its own demands as it was soon obvious that Herbert would have to live closer to his office. So another move was made, from Claremont and its hills to Murray Street, Perth.

> Murray Street! In this little cottage much happened. The front of our house, next but one to back entrance of Sir John Forrest's home. Was once invited to dance there to meet the first and only Duke of my life. Red, unattractive ... Wonder who he was!

Despite much happening they stayed but a relatively short time before making another move. This time it was across the Swan River to South Perth and into a large rambling house, 'The Dune', which was to be home for Cecie and Herbert for the remainder of their lives.

In Perth they gradually adapted to city life, although at weekends they regularly returned to the river and the bush.

The children were to feel the harshness of daily attendance at school, although education for May was to consist of a short term at Miss Best's School for Young Ladies, where classes provided her with little more than an audience for her humour and she drew praise from the teacher only for her map drawing. After the birth of a baby boy, Harold, a big disappointment to May who had wanted a sister, she was required to spend more time in the house to help her mother, so home was once again to provide her formal education. At the same time, her social life was stimulating as she was welcomed into the artistic circle in which her parents were prominent. But she recalled her favourite times were with her father on drawing excursions.

> My interest at that time was everything I saw and I was particularly keen on making fun of things.

Judge Hensman, a fine violinist, and his wife, a talented pianist, formed the Music Union and Cecilia Gibbs, her brother Ishmael and his wife were enthusiastic early members. The Union quickly gained prominence in Perth and they were encouraged to launch a Gilbert and Sullivan operetta. As a result, the Amateur Theatrical Society of Perth was established and May remembered the excitement which took over The Dune.

> My mother was the contralto and rehearsed her lines with a book propped up in the kitchen and her solos while scrubbing the family washing under the mulberry tree in our back yard.

May willingly took on more chores in the house and cared for baby Harold so that Cecie could spend time at rehearsals and, months later in St George's Hall, which boasted the only stage in town, the Amateur Theatrical Society presented *The Pirates of Penzance* for the citizens of Perth. It was May's first experience of a theatrical presentation, a magic memory for any teenager but typically for May it was remembered best for its humorous moments.

> With her magnificent voice and splendid sense of humour, my mother played a leading role and so did Chief Justice Onslow, a

> fine singer and player. This player forgot his lines, so Mother took him by the scruff and shook him to his great surprise and the delight of the audience.

Years later in London, she was to compare the local production with a professional presentation and her natural bias found her mother's company far superior.

> Our producer, Hart, was just out from London, where Gilbert and Sullivan had been going for a long time. He was slight and a marvellous actor, just made for those parts, whose singing, dancing, comedy and originality were all unique and perfect. Years later in London we saw the original [performer] who played these parts from the start, considered great stuff—it was flat and dull compared with our little masterpiece.

The practice sessions of the musical and theatrical societies generally involved the Gibbs household. Musicians and artists of the small colony regarded The Dune as a meeting place and it was in an atmosphere of happy artistic endeavour that May spent most

May, aged 16, in the chorus of The Gondoliers. *Amateur theatricals were an important part of family life in Perth.*

of her teenage years. As the daughter of two prominent members of Perth's artistic society, she was encouraged in the arts and urged to experiment. She painted set designs and acted as art director for many amateur productions and was highly praised for her work. At one stage, she fancied following in her mother's footsteps as a principal singer and so joined the South Perth Musical Society but, although her voice was good and strong, she never graduated beyond the 'ladies of the chorus'.

Despite her failure to gain a solo singing role, May showed promise in other areas of musical endeavour. Her violin tutor, Herr Franzick, who later became head of the Prague Conservatorium, found her a talented student and was disappointed when she eventually declared for her first love, art. Many years later, May was to say to an aspiring pupil, 'If you can leave art alone—sort of take it or leave it, it is not the real thing.'

The Dune boasted a large, bright area which was always referred to as 'Mr Gibbs' Studio' but gradually, always with the warm encouragement of 'the owner', it was May who took over the space with her prolific drawing. Still life and landscape were the fashionable themes of the day but May was experimenting with the human form and already she was revealing a penchant for capturing character. She was also, she recalled, exploring what made people laugh and was developing the off-beat humour which was later to distinguish her cartoons. May's sense of humour was not only restricted to her cartoons.

> When I was a girl, the climate being very hot we all used to take a rest. The bedrooms opened upon a veranda where pot plants and long coconut matting made a kind of pleasant passage.
>
> At about two o'clock the baker used to come in the side gate, walk briskly up the brick pathway to the edge of the veranda and called out 'Baggue'.
>
> My mother's drowsy voice would answer from inside her french windows.
>
> 'Two loaves please, baker.'
>
> 'Thanggue,' the baker would say putting the bread down on the rustic table.
>
> I used to hear this from my bedroom window nearby and it used to amuse me.
>
> One day I came in the side gate and walked heavily up the brick path to the veranda and called:
>
> 'Baggue.'

> 'Two loaves please, baker.'
>
> 'Thanggue,' I said.
>
> By and by the baker came walking briskly up the brick path to the veranda and called,
>
> 'Baggue.'
>
> 'Two loaves please, baker.'
>
> 'Thanggue,' said the baker.
>
> Later taking her cup of tea she said,
>
> 'Can't think what the baker was doing, he came twice—how many loaves did he leave?'

After an apprenticeship in watercolours, Herbert directed her in the initial stages of oil painting and May treated the new medium with positive aggression.

> Attacked oils—painting anything at all—trying to get beyond the sticky stage ... painting plaques to hang on walls and earning enough to keep myself in all but chemist bills.

Her life in the city was ideally balanced by her trips back to The Harvey, where she was always welcome. Uncle George had managed to wrest a living from the contrary Harvey soil and, although it was never the grand estate he envisaged when he urged his brother to come to Australia with him, George Gibbs and his wife Ellen established at Australind a fine pioneer home which still stands. These trips to The Harvey were always among May's happiest recollections. A comical note or card would announce her imminent arrival and the household would be abuzz with anticipation of entertainment, and the latest gossip from Perth.

May was a great favourite, not only with her aunt and uncle, but with her younger cousins. She found she had a gift for story-telling, not just an entertaining way of relating news, but an ability to weave a plot, and her cousins would be spellbound as she told her tales. The Harvey did not have an established school until 1896 and the Gibbs children had much the same style of education as May had had, so she also enjoyed teaching them. Remembering the wonders of her country childhood, she was able to reveal many secrets of the bush. Flat on their stomachs, the cousins large and small observed the ways of a busy ant; struggling up trees with a suitable foothold they peeked at baby birds; sitting as still as the lizard they watched, trying to outstare him as he matched his skin to his surroundings, thinking he had concealed his presence. Under May's guidance, the world opened up for the

Gibbs children—the first May Gibbs fans? For her part, she felt the satisfaction engendered by an appreciative audience.

The death of the eighteen-year-old Bertie from rheumatic fever was a sudden tragedy for the Gibbs family. May was in her mid-teens and Bertie's death was her first devastating loss. She felt it deeply. Captain Bertie was the hero of her earliest memories, the leader of the adventures on the sailing ship, the skipper of the bathtub fleet, her big brother, gone forever.

By the mid-1890s Perth was emerging from its embryonic state and becoming a bustling city. The gold rush of 1893 had attracted an influx of new hopefuls from all round the world. The population increased by over 50 per cent and business grew. Herbert Gibbs, now a settled member of the community, observed it all without envy. He had found his niche in Australia and was no longer chasing a dream. He and Cecie were busy with their artistic pursuits, Ivan was at Hale School, with Harold following all too rapidly behind him, and May was attending classes in the infant Art Gallery of Western Australia.

The social life of Perth by this time was an exciting one, particularly for young ladies, as there were two males to every female in Western Australia and beaux were readily available for daughters of marriageable age. But May showed no inclination towards romantic involvement, preferring the companionship of family acquaintances. Though expressing motherly concern, Cecie had to confess that her daughter lacked the qualities of an efficient housewife and her complete indifference to household routine hardly equipped her for the state of matrimony. Then there was May's indifference to the state of matrimony itself. While some men doubtless found May to be a young lady of warm personality and jolly conversation, others could have found themselves smarting at replies from her keen-edged tongue. May would wield a witticism with accuracy, a trait which did little to enhance her chances with gentlemen admirers.

It was May's adoration of her father that was in part responsible for her critical eye with regard to men, for Herbert was the yardstick by which they were all measured. She had adored her father from an early age and the comradeship between them developed much more strongly than it did between mother and daughter. She had yet to find anyone as companionable as her father.

Despite this seeming lack of interest in the opposite sex May's thoughts were definitely turning to romance and, in her twenty-first year, she began writing poetry.

It cannot last. It will not stay
Some breeze will blow it all away
And I shall love to love once more
And laugh and frivol as before.

And yet how long is there to sail?
Ah me — I would I knew my fate.
No, no I will be patient still
For after all it is God's will.

And I must learn as others do
That what seems hard is best
And those who still their duty do
Shall be forever blessed.

All I hold most dear on earth
All my life's ambitions worth
All is gone — gone from me
Tossing in the deep blue sea.

So many weary miles away
Far from here — where I must stay
Longing, longing — while he
Tossing further still from me.

Oh, I would the world were small
So that e'en the lightest call
Would bring him to me
Ah! I would there were no sea.

Yet all my grief may be in vain
For nothing all my weary pain
He may never think of me
Tossing in the deep blue sea.

The poems all had a melancholy note not found in any of her other work and were undoubtedly part of the selfconscious seriousness and drama of young adulthood. But May soon lost interest in such poetry and abandoned it for light-hearted verse, which she coupled with her humorous sketches.

My name is May
And I'm sorry to say
I have worked very hard
Doing nothing all day.

My family's away
And I have to stay
All by myself in this house
And I'm jolly well tired of it.

By my billy old self,
All the billy old day.

I know a girl she's round and fat.
She keeps a funny little cat.
And does not know
Most strange to say
No person's round and fat like May.

For that's the girl's name,
Don't you know.
I quite forgot to tell you so.

I'll get up on the fence—
How's that for high.
And stare at all the young men passing by

I like that sort of work don't you.
It is such easy work to do.

While Herbert and Cecie waited for May to show some indication of settling down and marrying, teachers at the art gallery were suggesting that she should be sent to art school in England. This resulted in much debate in the family circle for, apart from Herbert's lack of funds to finance such a move, there were doubts regarding the stability of a female artist's career.

Perhaps the mood of Western Australia itself helped in the decision making. The suffragette movement, which had been active in the state for some time, won an unexpected victory. The Western Australian government of the day gave women the right to vote, mistakenly believing that they would tip the balance for a 'no' vote against Federalism. When the women's vote supported Federalism, the suffragette movement and freedom for women became topics of conversation throughout Perth. Careers for women became not only more readily acceptable but also more available as a result of the state's participation in the Boer War. Women were encouraged to become involved in pursuits in which they had never previously participated.

In this atmosphere, May, at twenty-two, decided to go to England to study and after much deliberating, it was agreed that she could make the trip and begin her studies in the new year.* The men were to be left in the care of Butsie, their housekeeper and family friend, so that Cecie could accompany May, together with a cousin, Daisy Rogers.

With good intentions May started a diary.

> We left Fremantle aboard *Konigin Luise* on February 21st at 4.30 p.m., and gradually steamed into rougher sea. By the following morning, when I scrambled up the deck in a loose wrapper with only shoes on my feet, the sea was running high and a stiff wind was blowing and also my hair for I had (such was the distress of my feelings) quite given up all idea of any toilet—even the vainest girl forgets personal appearances the first two or three days on board.
>
> Having resigned myself to fate on a deck chair, I watched the sailor hosing and scrubbing the deck and would have stayed to be washed away had not a dear man with a brown beard and twinkling good natured eyes come to my rescue and hoisted me and my chair on to the top of a hatchway where he had his own chair—so he talked to me and I tried to feel better—that day was not a success.

* When interviewed, the elderly May recalled four trips to England, but her writings and drawings only document three trips, in 1900, 1904 and 1909. During the period suggested by some for an earlier visit, 1896–1898, there is evidence that May was in Perth.

5
ENGLAND REVISITED

Sir X comes in, a big quiet man with a nice manner, but I think he is bored with us. He looks at my sketches and advises 'Cope & Nichol' school at South Kensington.

This Other Fair(y) Tale,
notes for autobiography

May Gibbs' return trip across the Indian Ocean in 1900 was not nearly as exciting as her maiden voyage as a four-year-old. She and her mother shared a cabin in third class where the conditions could hardly have been more comfortable than they had been eighteen years previously.

> I came to the conclusion that no one but a helpless fool would, could endure it and tumbled out, staggered along the passage, dragging my dressing gown as I went, regardless and indifferent to everything but the one mad desire to get out of such an inferno.

Some relief was had in the tropics by following the age-old tradition of sleeping on deck.

> On Friday the 29th, Mother and I spent the night out on the deck in preference to the small hell—I mean the cabin. We had rugs and cushions and made a hard but deliciously cool and fresh bed on the top of a large hatchway.

Many of the passengers and crew were captured in her sketch book, which she kept by her side throughout the trip, and some were also recorded in her diary.

> We made friends with a jolly frisky little German—French girl, Miss Frochine, who has spent several hours on our deck and a Miss Wiseman, a charming girl, is one of us.

During this journey there also emerged the first likely beau for the young Miss Gibbs. Towards the latter part of the voyage, she spent most of her time in the company of a young man in his late twenties and, although their association can only have been brief as he left the ship in Genoa, arrangements were made for them to meet again in London. Apparently Cecie was not happy about the gentleman's interest in her daughter, which is somewhat puzzling since she had been more than a trifle concerned about May's complete lack of enthusiasm for romantic attachments back home. When he eventually attempted to pursue the friendship in London, the suitor was greeted very coldly by Cecie who also admonished May for not getting enough rest. May had contracted German measles soon after arriving in England and was still convalescent. The young couple made a visit together to the Royal Academy and he called two or three times to enquire about her health. On his last visit, apparently restricted by the presence of Mrs Gibbs, he slipped May a note asking her to meet him the following night. May waited and he did not appear and she was not to see him again. May suspected her mother's interference was responsible for the disappearance of her friend and for some time relations were strained between the two women.

On their arrival in England, they had headed for the Rogers' headquarters in Cheam Fields, Surrey. For Cecie, this must have been a joyous reunion with so many relatives but May soon tired of the family reminiscences and spent most of her time walking in the English countryside. She was fascinated by its contrast to the Australian bush and produced many watercolours during this sojourn in Surrey. Her notes are full of her pleasure in her surroundings.

> It was spring and we stayed at the quaintest cottage. By the roadside, I saw my first English wild violets and blue bells, thick as grass spread under the fir trees, but it was freezing.
>
> The house clung to a lane which swayed and came to a main road, along which an occasional wonder, an automobile, thundered in a whirl of dust or splatter of mud, scattering the chicks. Elms and hedges fenced the lane, the elms trousered in small branches from ground to some 12 feet up.

With a letter of introduction to one of the fashionable artists of the day May submitted some of her sketches and was accepted into one of the better London art schools, the Cope and Nichol in South Kensington. So began a concentrated program which was exhausting but at the same time extraordinarily stimulating. A half-hour train ride and ten-minute walk was followed by seven hours of intense sketching, with barely a lunch break, six days a week. At the end of the day, the pupils left their sketches for the approval or otherwise of Mr Nichol, their teacher, who would pass on his comments the following day.

In the following weeks, May was conscious of nothing but art. The long sessions at the school were followed by sketching and painting at home and no other interest could capture her attention. When the class commenced working with models, she became engrossed in the human form, and fascinated by the challenge of every individual face. At the end of the day, she found herself unconsciously studying her companions in the train until they became embarrassed or annoyed at her scrutiny.

Evidently satisfied that her daughter was now safely absorbed in her studies, Cecie returned to Australia, leaving May on her own for the first time. Her dedication to her work continued and she kept her family regularly informed of her progress.

> I have had some praise for my work from Mr Nichol and some of the girls. Mr Nichol merely said I was 'all right' and that I was getting on 'very well, very well' and his visit was short which means that you are getting on favourably and do not need his help. Do not worry, Father, I shall get on. I have all the faith in myself but no conceit—just simply that I feel sure of what I shall be able to do with earnest hard work. I find my work my greatest pleasure and Sundays are very tedious. I am always glad when Monday comes again.

If May had had any illusions about her new freedom, they were quickly dispelled by the realisation that, in addition to her work, she now had to look after herself, so her schedule became even heavier. At the same time, she was aware of the immense value of the concentrated study.

> ... this steady work every day soon tells. I feel far more at home with my charcoal point than I did when I began. It used to do what it liked with me once.

And a further report of praise by the normally reticent Mr Nichol:

> ... the students were so astonished that he had said so much, it was such a rare thing for Mr Nichol. Now, aren't you pleased? He has advised me to go for the Academy—that is to try and work up, then send in some work at the examination time, but that will not be just yet and I'll have to do lots more work I expect.

In fact, in the coming months she was to display a concentration and speed which greatly impressed her tutors. On their recommendations and encouragement, she expanded her studies by attending night classes at the Chelsea Polytechnic Institute. This necessitated a move to the city and, with the help of fellow students, she found a room in Marguerite Terrace, off Oakley Street, Chelsea. Although in a relatively poor area, it was close to the Polytechnic and the rent was reasonable, a consideration now that she had to pay for her night classes.

Her stay in Chelsea began with an unsettling incident when the landlady and her cab-driver husband absconded one night with the rent and the owners refused to give May her mail until the outstanding rent was paid.

May Gibbs had made good friends at her school and there was a pleasant companionship between the students and teachers. Occasionally there was horseplay—a bread fight, a hockey game or a prank played on some innocent victim. May's contribution to the levity was verses and a sketch dashed off and pinned to the subject's easel. But time for relaxation and fun was becoming increasingly rare and, when the Christmas break came, she welcomed the invitation to stay at her Aunt Ada's in Surrey.

The Rogers family had dutifully kept an eye on May and regularly sent her invitations to attend their gatherings. Feeling she could not participate in these and keep up with her work, she had refused most offers but now, in the warmth of Aunt Ada's home, she realised how she had missed good food, comfortable surroundings and fresh country air. They, in turn, could see that she was suffering from overwork and lack of an adequate diet and determined to restore her to good health. In the weeks that followed she was lovingly spoiled. She also found great relaxation playing with the children, weaving stories for them as she had for her cousins at The Harvey, and developing an alphabet book for the younger ones.

By the time she returned to London May was ready to resume her studies and these were to continue for a further twelve months.

On her twenty-fourth birthday, 17 January 1901, May's thoughts were with her father. The student reported to the teacher of her childhood with her second pencil drawing done at the 'Poly':

> I would send some charcoal drawings but feel it would be imposing too much on little Daisy.
>
> This is not nearly so good as my charcoal, but being small I could send them. You can see I'm not used to this pencil work yet and the

> paper wants knowing. This is the paper B. Johnson always uses and advocates. One more excuse for myself, I had a vile pencil which I would insist on using for the sake of economy.
>
> I shall soon be sending some more work out to show you how I can improve on this—I've great hope of getting on so 'Hurrah' in spite of these poor specimens.

During the twelve months of 1901, May handled a variety of styles of art work—fine line, pen, charcoal and pencil sketching. Every day there were models for costume drawing, character sketching and that elusive form, the nude.

There was again little time for recreation. As well as night classes May, like all struggling artists, visited those institutions where, because of a patron's generosity, studies for half-hour poses were free. The Albert and Victoria Studios in South Kensington was one of these.

> I went to lots of night schools, which were rather fun. You never knew what you'd come on in a night school.

It was a year of concentrated work and her intense dedication led to a lack of interest in her personal welfare. By the end of 1901, her health started to deteriorate as the London fogs proved dangerous to her lungs and she found herself suffering from recurring chills. Finally her concerned parents persuaded her to return and she boarded a vessel for home.

It was undoubtedly a decision she regretted. As soon as the excitement of the homecoming was over and she had completed the round of relatives and friends, May was restless. She longed for London and grew critical of everything Australian, including the strong accent. Herbert, who by now considered himself a true Australian, was particularly hurt by her behaviour.

Having decided to seek work as an illustrator, May began the rounds of the newspapers but found that the professionals were solidly entrenched and that there was little interest in the work of a female artist. Eventually, one editor, after perusing her work, thought she might be able to handle some illustrations for the retail stores' fashion advertisements. It was hardly the type of work she had envisaged but she accepted it.

Following the success of this assignment, Herbert used his influence for May to gain some assignments with a Western Australian magazine, the *Social Kodak*. This was more interesting work as it gave her the opportunity for social comment. Her identity was concealed behind the pseudonym 'Blob', a nickname from an old family joke and, on one occasion, her directness caused one politician to threaten to take action against the 'upstart' hiding behind a pen-name. May was quite anxious to accept the challenge but her family pointed out the problems this would create in a small community, so she remained anonymous. 'Ann Onymous' was the name May Gibbs always intended to use on her proposed autobiography.

While the illustrations helped her to earn an income, May continued her studies by having members of the family sit for her. Ivan seems the only one to have escaped as Herbert, Cecie and Harold, plus numerous relatives, feature largely in the collection of sketches she did during this period. She even coaxed Butsie, their housekeeper and a particularly close friend, to model in the nude and the result is a very dejected subject, the sketch accurately capturing Butsie's discomfort.

It would appear that the first interest in material for children manifested itself during this period. In discussions with her parents, May decried the lack of material for children and experimented by taking known nursery rhymes and adapting them to a fantasyland with an Australian background. She portrayed her mother as 'The Old Woman Who Lived in a Hat', surrounding her with beetle-like gnomes for servants. And it was at this time that May made her first experiments using Australian animals (more correctly, fish) with human characteristics in a story with illustrations called *John Dory, His Story*. Nothing came of the story but John's fearsome head was later to emerge in Little Ragged Blossom's adventures.

During this period, she was to spend a good deal of time with Jim Calanchini, an Australian-Italian born in Victoria. Calanchini worked with Herbert and Ivan at the Lands Department and was to become a close friend, a member of the extended Gibbs family for the rest of his life. He fell in love with May and, although she did not return his affection, she enjoyed talking to him about London and the exciting art world she had known.

The lure of London was to prove too strong and, three years after returning home, May sailed for England on the ss *Afric* in 1904, again accompanied by her cousin, Daisy Rogers, who was making one of her regular visits to her mother and sister.

Marguerite Terrace was once more to provide living quarters and this time she shared the accommodation with Daisy.

May immediately enrolled at the Chelsea Polytechnic and also at Mr Henry Blackburn's School for Black and White Artists, 123 Victoria Street, Westminster.

> The constant clicking of the horses' feet chomping down floated up to the school at the top of the building and Victoria Street provided a rhythm that was hard to block out.

This school was the first of its kind in London and excelled in the tuition of single-line drawing. Line work was just growing in popularity and May attributed her success with this style to the quality and quantity of copy work she had done as a child.

> Single line so splendidly used by Ralph Caldecott in his children's books was my delight and must have helped me as I was so often copying his pages as a child.

She also attended Mary Woodward's Little Studios at Chelsea where the models were children and was to find a special delight in these assignments. But, with the night classes for her nude tuition, it was back to the old routine of ten-hour days so there could be little time for relaxation.

> Every day up the stairs I would go. Some days we worked from original black and white line drawings by celebrated artists, some days costume models and every day was work, work, work. We had splendid practice in all different styles.

At the Chelsea Polytechnic, she was briefly under the tutelage of the awesome Augustus John, whom she dismissed with typical candour.

> The night class-master was Augustus John, who looked like a picture of Christ dressed in a checked suit, velvet collar, long tailed coat, large ear rings, no shirt, just a pullover jersey. I disliked him and his nudes which were framed and hanging around the walls of the two rooms. His models were very fat.

We do not know what Augustus John thought of May Gibbs but, after a half-dozen classes under his supervision, she returned to her sketching in Borough Johnson's classes. Johnson had been an encouraging tutor from her earliest days at the Polytechnic. He had been impressed by her tremendous capacity for work and was

May in Herbert Gibbs's studio at The Dune, Perth, 1904.

to have a great influence on her. He was also aware of her driving ambition and sympathised, knowing what a treacherous path an artist's life was for anyone, and especially for a woman. At the end of her stay at the Blackburn school and the Chelsea Polytechnic, May was to receive first class passes in every category and her term at Mr Henry Blackburn's School for Black and White Artists was to decide the direction which her career would take.

The Blackburn school was an excellent reference as it was a source of skilled artists for the magazines, newspapers and publishing houses of England but she was only one of the large group of talented people applying for the jobs available. There was also that other barrier to overcome. While women in Australia had the vote the suffragette movement in England was still fighting for the right to vote, and its militancy made the male population even more cautious and resistant to career women. Those who felt their jobs threatened were not receptive to applications from females for the few positions available. Illustrating was a man's domain!

May had yet to test the strength of these barriers when, in April 1905, Cecie arrived in London with Harold who was to attend school there. Their arrival seemed to prompt May to run away again. Perhaps she was not enthusiastic about the prospects of sharing a tiny flat with her mother and brother or perhaps living in close proximity prompted the quarrels which so easily erupted between Cecie and May. For whatever reason, May Gibbs turned once more back to Australia, having failed yet again to really establish herself as an artist.

May's parents, Cecilia and Herbert Gibbs, in Perth, 1905.

6
THE ILLUSTRATOR

I've just remembered a few things that I thought of the other day. People have more wrinkles here than they do in England. Most of the trees are tall, cats are tall and thin, so are horses and even pigs. People talk in a tall thin way — lots of flowers are tall and thin. Snakes are long and thin and so are lizards. Flies are not and there are millions of them.

Story Notes from a Sketchbook

On her return to Perth in 1905, May was to embark on a successful career as an illustrator for Western Australia's leading newspaper, the *Western Mail*. The editor, Robert Robertson, was married to author and outspoken leader of women's rights Agnes Robertson who, after seeing May's work, arranged an interview with her husband. Robertson was delighted with the professional polish displayed by the young artist and commissioned May to illustrate the front page of the 1905 Christmas issue. Her patriotic presentation of the western state drew much favourable comment and ensured a regular flow of commissions from the newspaper.

A contemporary of May once described her as 'a body burdened with talents' and indeed she had yet to discover the field in which her talents could be given full rein. Now, with the financial security from her *Western Mail* assignments, she commenced to dabble in other creative arts.

After a visit in Perth to a theatre company production of *Charley's Aunt*, which she had illustrated in the local newspaper, May turned to short story writing. The heroine of these stories was Fay, who always featured as the toast of the town and won the hearts of all about her except for those of May's family and friends who were unimpressed. Undeterred, May turned to play writing and devised a drama around the adventures of the glamorous Fay in the Kalgoorlie goldfields. The only person to encourage these endeavours was Herbert who contributed to the devising of plot and characterisation discussion. May eventually grew tired of the project and abandoned it.

Her drawings of this period include the development of a number of ideas, most notably a series of illustrations called the

Queer People which make comic comment on human frailties. There were, too, further experiments wherein Australian animals assume human characteristics. These feature in a half-finished manuscript titled *Nursery Rhymes from the Bush.* It is interesting to note that her hero and heroine in this book were pleasant snakes—far removed from the venomous Mrs Snake who later schemes her way through *Snugglepot and Cuddlepie.*

She continued to write, interminably scribbling in notebooks and on scraps of paper—poetry, prose, story ideas and odd letters to herself under different guises for changing moods.

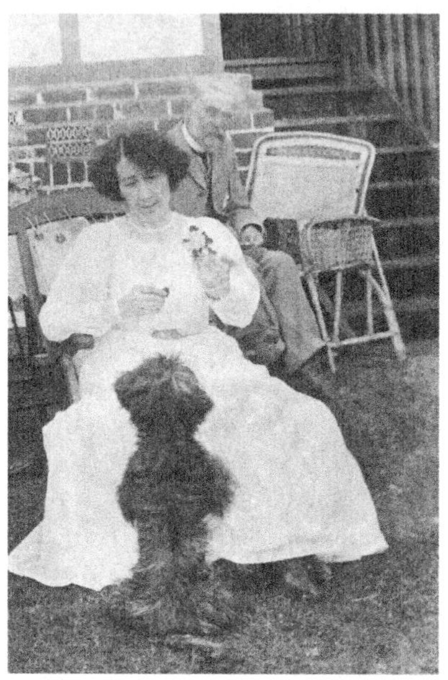

May with 'Wog' who featured in her stories 'Mimie and Wog' (unpublished) and 'About Us' (published in 1911).

In the Soulhouse of the Lady of Moods—Thursday Night.

Dear Mr Builder,

You don't know me perhaps? May I introduce myself—Nurse Commonsense. I don't live in this soulhouse but I come to nurse the Lady of the Words sometimes—Dr Reason generally employs me for his patients.

> The Lady of the Words is very sick—we have had the doctors to her. Dr Time (nice old chap but somewhat old-fashioned), Dr Introspection and my doctor. They are all agreed on one point. The patient is in a very serious condition.
>
> The house is closed and the knocker tied up and a load of hay has been put outside on the road.
>
> As the Lady of Moods is very fond of me perhaps more so than I am of her, I thought it only proper that I should warn her close friends of her critical state. She may die at any moment.
>
> Her illness is a puzzle to the doctors.

The patient did not die but recovered to compile an adventure book, titled *Mimie and Wog, Their Adventures in Australia*, 'Told and Pictured by Silvia Hood', another pseudonym. Written for very young children, it tells the story of Mimie and her ever-faithful companion, Wog, a dog of doubtful heritage. Months were spent on the manuscript and illustrations which the family and friends agreed had originality and charm. Calanchini was the only one to raise a doubt about the nudity of the heroine and wondered if it would be acceptable to the public. May, in turn, threatened to sketch a nude study of her critic if he continued on about the 'unclothed figure', as she preferred to describe her creation.

There were very few publishers in Perth at this time and those to whom she submitted *Mimie and Wog* failed to agree with her that there was a need for an adventure book. Disappointed, she put it aside and concentrated on her newspaper work, but *Mimie and Wog* was, in retrospect, the beginning.

For a while, Agnes Robertson interested May in illustrating works with a message for the women's rights movement. 'Women's Position in the State' by 'One of Them' was a strong article appearing in the *Western Mail* in 1907. The article deplored the status of women in Western Australia and enticed the more adventurous to broaden their horizons and seek their fortunes in an exciting world away from the restrictions of their home state. May was in sympathy with the article, obviously thinking once again of London, but she was never a dedicated feminist, even though on many occasions her work was commissioned by the women's movement. As she said, many years later, 'I never thought of myself other than as an individual and I was never anti-man.'

The Dune was still a social centre and the Gibbs, now one of the better known families of Perth, had settled down to a pleasant existence. Herbert made his weekday trips to the Lands Department, where his work admittedly came second to his interest in art and silversmithing. Cecie was back from London once more. Harold too was home and enjoying what he considered a well-earned holiday after a year's English schooling, and Ivan held a position at Elders, now one of the largest agricultural business houses in Western Australia.

When May found life at The Dune too routine, she escaped to Uncle George's farm at The Harvey, just as she had done a decade earlier, and the duration of her stay seemed to grow longer with each visit. The Harvey brought her back to the Australian countryside which she was always to find a source of rejuvenation and inspiration.

Once again the cousins provided her with a youthful audience on whom to test her storytelling skills and from whom she received valuable reminders about children's preoccupations and interests. The sophisticated Miss Gibbs of Perth had little other direct contact with children either then or in later years yet she remained consistently in touch with her young audience.

A highlight of one of her more lengthy visits to The Harvey was her cousin Len's twenty-first birthday party. As a special surprise May prepared a gallery of caricatures and the Gibbs family watched delighted as their neighbours came to life under May's clever hand. Birdie Gibbs was only ten years of age at the time and, many years later, she told her daughter Marian the story.

> Mamie did caricatures of lots of the locals. When the guests at the party saw the gallery of pictures, they laughed and commented on May's talent to capture the subject's dominating features, but when confronted with their own portrait, a false laughter replaced their mirth. Many neighbours were displeased when they left but later they too could see the fun in their own particular picture and the following morning found an excuse to visit the Gibbs in the hope of enticing Miss Gibbs to part with the drawings. To their dismay they found the artist had destroyed every one of her sketches.

In entertaining her friends, May had also offended them and was quick to remove the cause of the embarrassment.

The Gibbs of Harvey became subjects for another idea which came to life around this period. Realising how little was known on the other side of the world about Australia, she depicted life in an Australian country district, using her relatives and their neighbours as prototypes, in correspondence between two pen friends, Tom from the imaginary Australian town, Cooligicup, and Bob in Switzerland. The letters reveal an interesting record of life on the farm in 1907.

Dear Bob,

There are lots of people at Cooligicup, the old Way-backers, like Mike Doonan, some who have been working men and got a bit and then there are the New Chums ...

Dear Bob,

I am sorry I missed last mail ... we had a sudden encounter with a bushfire ... we kept up going as hard as we could from about 12 till half past 4 ... a great big lizard ran up Jim as if he were a tree, he let out a yell ... I happened to have my gun and shot it ... It's rather a dangerous life.

Dear Bob,

... Goodbye tinned milk—we've got a cow—she's a great little bit—Tony milks her. She goes for him sometimes—I would do it only mother won't let me ...
Dear Bob,

... You're a corker, I did laugh when I read your letter. Just fancy thinking Black Boys were men ... they're sort of black trees with green and yellow grass growing out of the top.

Dear Bob,

The mosquitoes are awful. And that noise—I don't think I told you—it's quite ghostly—there's something in the roof, it walks about on the ceiling at night—sounds like a crocodile or a big monkey—Father says it's a rat ... Aunt Peg says it's a possum—Jim says it's a lizard. This is Aunt Peg, that's just like a woman—women can't argue but they always want to. She's not a bad old stick—she smokes.

Dear Bob,

... This is another thing I noticed ... the bush is sad—sad and strange—most of the flowers are queer shapes—nearly all have hard stiff leaves—they are beautiful but strange too—then most of the noises of the bush are sad or strange—the native dog howls at night in a way to make you shudder. The curlew gives you cold

> shivers down your back—the Morepork (a bird) is as mournful as mud, and there are heaps of other queer sounds in the bush, the constant shrieking of the cicada is one—something like a sea of policemen's whistles ...
>
> Dear Bob,
>
> ... Jim and I are burning the logs—we blast them first— There's bush right up to the house on one side. You should see the snakes and reptiles and things we burn out—tons of them.
> ... I've got a little Joey Kangi—Jim shot its mother.

This notebook, full of words and illustrations of an era long past, ends with May's thoughts on the bush.

This then was May Gibbs in 1909, at the age of thirty-two. Her life was pleasant, she was earning a comfortable living with her assignments, although not accomplishing all she would have liked. She was talented, liked her independence, loved children, enjoyed male companionship and hated housekeeping. She had few attachments, loved her father, had petty quarrels with her mother, was affectionate towards her brothers and enjoyed the companionship of the large circle of relatives and friends.

Marriage was certainly a possibility as the male population in Western Australia continued to far outnumber the female and widows rarely remained single for long. However, May was 'not the kind that could take it'. She was suspicious of the state of matrimony, considering that most men were looking for a servant and bed companion. She was a romantic but at this time dismissed the possibility of romance in her life. A notebook jotting reveals something of her then ambivalent feelings about the opposite sex.

Man do you stand for evil
A something out of place?
Or are you Tonic poison
In the Blood of Human Race?

She was not a beautiful woman, her heavy features and wiry hair giving her a rather unfeminine appearance, but she was certainly more attractive than she depicted herself. Her self-portraits were always unflattering caricatures and these she distributed almost daily in the hand-sketched postcards she sent to friends.

Thus when cupid appeared at this time it was only in May's imagination in a series of cartoons and verse which mock the marriage conventions of the day. May's cherub has trouble piercing the hearts of the materialistic and selfish with his tiny darts. None of this material was ever published and what is presented here is in its unedited manuscript form.

There are some great and tender men
I love them all their lives
And o'it grieves me when I find
I've muddled up their wives

They say I'm blind but that's not so
I see them all as round they go
I shoot at random that is true
The game is better when I do

Old Maid come off your dusty shelf these
are the days of hope
You still may tie the marriage knot there's lots
and lots of rope
I've got some husbands coming on they won't
take long to grow
To marry when you're very very old's
the fashion now you know.
To a Bachelor with a generous mind,
a susceptible heart and a large purse

Be careful of your big heart — don't leave it hanging out.
Some one will surely see it if you leave it so about
Some/A thief will come and take it leave you hers instead —
But yours is a golden heart and hers will be but red.

One further piece of May's imaginative writing of the time survives in a letter to her relation Winifred Preston and preserves better than her literary efforts of the period, her humour and spirit. The letter also reveals that May had plans to go to London.

'The Dune'
South Perth
July 19th.09

Dear Aunt Winny

With no maid—at least only an 'Old Maid' (groans) and one Mother with a lumbago back—to do the house work you can guess how much time hangs heavy on my hands—every mail I've been going to catch. You've had a narrow escape I very nearly accepted your invitation to come and stay—I'd like to see what it feels like to have 1 & a $\frac{1}{2}$ servants all to myself—that's about how it pans out in your household as far as I can see—the dress you sent me doesn't like its new position at all and is decidedly sniffy and stuck up. I heard it complain to my 4 year old (best) tweed—that she'd seen better days and wasn't used to mixing in such low company—'such worn out old frumps'. The 40 year old silk tried to rustle and show some spirit but only succeeded in tumbling off her hook where she lay with one of her biggest holes upwards—one that had been darned too—poor thing. Anyhow the newcomer is not having a rosy time and turned very pale when she heard me tell a friend I was going to have in my Dr—Mrs Mcin Attire—to perform an operation on her—but when she understood that it would make a new woman of her and that dinners and theatre would result she became reconciled.

It is going to be my coming out, my 21st, no—41st—no, I've forgotten—now you'll know—I'm in the period when you *do* forget!! Anyhow the frock's going to be so useful and I love the colour and you're a dear like 'Nell dear' as I always call that darling, lovely woman, I love (with two capital L's) Aunt Nell—If I've a dress decent enough (I won't go out if I haven't clothes) I'll come and see you when you come to England—if you'd like me to? It's a piece of vanity of mine—not to go where I'm not really wanted—quite wanted—Life's too short—too full—to be wasted on duty visits and it isn't fair to anyone. Mother has told me lots about you and little Mabel and your home—I'd love to come—anyhow I hope to see you in London. I'd like to do the watercolours—only the flowers are not out and I'm likely to be gone before they are—Kangaroos are out—do you want them? How would you like blue Leschenaultia, the best of all the W.A. wild flowers?

With much love to you.
And Mabel too.
May

May's work remained her main motivation in life yet while her portfolio was growing she must have felt disappointment in the direction of her career. *Mimie and Wog* and the nursery rhyme book in which she had invested much hope had both failed to find a publisher. Added to this came the unexpected challenge of competition. Since she had usurped Ben Strange's position as the illustrator of the front page of the *Western Mail* Christmas issue she considered it her own domain and was quite unprepared for the announcement that she was to be replaced. Her successor was Ida S. Rentoul, a young Australian illustrator with no training but a great talent. Her wispy fairies and witches had become popular and were to find their own place in Australian children's literature.

'The barometer is low', May's self mocking Christmas card to a close friend reported, but the cancellation of the Christmas page was the final straw. As revealed in her letter to 'Aunt Winny', she had always planned to return to England. It seemed an ideal solution to go straight away. To cover her disappointment and embarrassment, she gave, as an excuse, that she wished to contact London publishers personally regarding her children's books. Only she promised herself that this would be her last attempt to succeed in London.

Once more, Cecie felt obliged to make the journey with her and to see her safely settled in London, an obligation which must have irritated and embarrassed the thirty-two year old, and in November 1909 they sailed on the steamer *Persic*, accompanied by yet another cousin, Evangeline.

7
RUNNING AWAY

'That's nonsense Nan, every girl when she reaches our age should strike out for herself, she needs freedom and wants to shape her life her own way. The dearest parents in the world are tyrants in that respect. Besides, you know well enough that my work is here.'

From Thoughts at a Boarding House,
notes for a story

On arrival in London, Cecie and May followed the now familiar routine of a holiday with the ever-welcoming Rogers family. May's happiness and optimism of this time is recorded in a notebook verse.

In Cheam Fields

The inner side of every cloud
Is bright and shining
So I turn my clouds about
And always wear them inside out
To show the lining

Then Cecie checked out London accommodation for her daughter. She finally settled her into St Albans, a young women's pension which catered for the very rich and very fashionable and to which young continental ladies were sent to learn the social graces. It was run by a High Church of England order and it appealed to May's sense of humour that, in the midst of this modest gentility, the Vicar's name was Father Hogg and one of the priests was a Father Suckling.

Cecie hoped that, in the regimented routine of St Albans, May would be assured of regular meals and comfortable accommodation. She was disturbed by the pattern which invariably followed May's visits to London—the overwork, the missing of meals, the tiredness which generally led to a breakdown in her health. Despite assurances to her mother, when May realised her funds were being depleted too quickly, she left St Albans and, for a short time, lived in a number of lodgings—church hostels, flatettes, the

YWCA, before finally settling in a small attic room high among the rooftops of London.

Her approaches to British publishers all resulted in the familiar rejection of her work but, in offering her some advice, one of the managers advised her to appoint an agent. On further recommendation, she placed her material with Charles H. Wood of 190 Fleet Street, and he, in turn, arranged an interview for her with George Harrap & Company, a small publishing house producing deluxe publications. When presented with May Gibbs' portfolio, Harrap expressed surprise at the range of her artistic skills and immediately contracted her to illustrate a book titled *Georgian England.*

This was the beginning. The forty-pound fee was a small fortune. With her usual perfectionism, May plunged into the research and found herself back in an old haunt of her student days, the British Museum with its library of books on period costume and furniture. A manuscript had been provided to the artist, revealing the action of the story. May's illustrations were to provide the atmosphere. Her ability to dramatise an event or incident greatly

May and Aunt Emily at Kew Gardens in 1911, during one of May's visits to England. Aunt Emily's home was a meeting place for the Australian and English members of the Rogers family.

supported the rather pedestrian storytelling and the painstaking research she carried out ensured her pictures were authentic.

While May brought to life the great moments in Georgian England, her agent tried to interest publishers in the children's books she had now assembled—*Nursery Rhymes from the Bush, Mimie and Wog, Their Adventures in Australia, Mimie and Wog in Fishland* and *John Dory*—but the stories failed to attract the London publishers.

No one was interested in tales of Australia, with its strange forests and wildlife. The creatures she depicted were unfamiliar and the constant reaction she received was, 'We need something with an English setting.'

There is no question that May's attack on the English publishing world was much more positive with one assignment to her credit. Instead of smarting under the criticism, she analysed it and realised it was only the setting of her stories which was unacceptable. She had confidence in their appeal, so she set about changing the setting and the characters.

Mimie and Wog, Their Adventures in Australia was the first story she tackled and, for good luck, she changed the heroine's name to Mamie. Mamie now became a neatly pretty and golden-haired English girl, rather than the somewhat scruffy denizen of outback Australia she had been in the original. Instead of the bushland, Mamie's adventures took her from the safety of her big white house and quiet garden to the hostile, fog-bound London streets of the early 1900s. Chimney Pot Land, where her story was set, was alive with creatures of the gutter, scraggy cats, smoking chimney pots and bare attics. The London fog was endowed with its own personality and was called The Smuts, bat-like creatures that constantly threatened Mamie and Wog. It is interesting that, from her early drawings, bats were sometimes featured as threats or obstacles and these creatures often appeared in the development of a new work.

The rewrite was successful and, under the title, *About Us,* the story was published by Ernest Nister in London and E. P. Dutton & Company in New York. Unfortunately it was not published in Australia. May received twenty pounds for the work, but there was no demand for a sequel, so she was forced to concentrate on Georgian England.

While waiting for publication May had spent the Christmas of 1910 with Aunt Emily at Wimbledon. It was a welcome holiday. May, as usual, was pampered by her relatives with the luxuries she had to deny herself. Aunt Emily's home was a meeting place for the Australian and English members of the Rogers family and, during this holiday period, May painted a delightful portrait of a child, Alice Hadfield.

Also at Wimbledon was her Australian relative Winifred Preston. The two women had finally met and 'Aunt Winny' was to become one of May's dearest friends. A talented painter herself, Win was financially independent and painted only for her own pleasure. She was very fond of the younger artist and always deeply interested in her progress. Together with her daughter Mabel, and son Ken, Win Preston took May to all the West End shows and events in London and made sure she enjoyed her holiday break. Finally, rejuvenated in health and spirit, May returned to her lodgings in the New Year.

Her agent arranged a number of assignments as an illustrator to various newspapers, and for the *Christian Commonwealth* she illustrated public debates, a then popular forum for the airing of contentious issues. One famous debate covered was on women's suffrage and was between Miss Cicely Hamilton and G. K. Chesterton. Years later, May Gibbs recalled the occasion:

> The small Queen's Hall was filled and I had to stand leaning against the wall, one knee up to hold my book while I sketched. G. B. Shaw was sitting a few rows from me.
>
> Cicely Hamilton was a novelist and writer of feminist plays and destined to become a representative of women's rights at the League of Nations. Her manner was intensely nervous and she had a way of flinging down her soul as a gauntlet, that would have put her at the mercy of any debater keener on scoring points and less like Mr Chesterton, a happy philosopher revelling in his own philosophy.
>
> Miss Hamilton introduced herself as thirty years of age and unmarried and when I looked about the crowd, I realised there were a lot of us in the same state.

May Gibbs' debate illustrations were to catch the attention of the editor of a women's paper, a publication with the depressing title *The Common Cause, The Organ of the National Union of Women's Suffrage Societies.* Once again, she found herself involved in the women's movement, though it was as an observer rather than a participant.

On completion and delivery of the Georgian England assignment, George Harrap expressed their pleasure by offering her another assignment. It was a similar type of book titled *The Struggle with the Crown*, which May was happy to accept. She believed she could now establish a routine for this type of work, which might make the next assignment easier.

For light relief from history and social upheaval, May worked again on the cupid themes and more adventures for Mamie and Wog, taking her two published characters through the land of the Arabian Nights and some fanciful nightmares. She was also again attending night classes, continuing as a pupil with Borough Johnson.

It was during this period that May was to meet the person who was virtually to share much of her life. Rene Heames was an English girl who was lodging at the same rooming house and, from their first meeting, they became close friends. Rene was employed at the telephone exchange in London and was an active socialist, being a member of the National Union of Women's Suffrage Societies. Thus feminist issues of the day were a natural topic of conversation and Rene must have been intrigued that May could so succinctly express women's problems in her cartoons and yet lacked the motivation for further involvement.

It is obvious from May's sketchbook notations of the time that Rene set about taking care of May as far as she was able. But, as always, May forgot to eat regularly and did not get enough rest and this careless disregard for her health, coupled with the damp London weather which had never been kind to her, again brought on a dose of bronchitis. When it looked like developing into pneumonia, Rene took action. There was little she could personally do to alleviate May's condition, because her financial situation was not much better than May's, but she had met Win Preston and her daughter, Mabel, and when a doctor warned that May was practically consumptive, Rene contacted the Prestons.

Without hesitation, and riding over her niece's protests, Win directed her chauffeur to scoop the frail body up in an enormous possum rug and they left the dingy quarters for the Queen Anne's Mansions. Here, with daily visits from the doctor, good food and a regular whisky to boost her spirits, she quickly recovered.

As soon as Win considered her well enough to travel, May was sent for a holiday to the English Lakes District in the care of Mabel and Ken. The holiday was recorded in a series of postcards May drew and sent to Win and they eloquently express her happiness during this period.

Leaving London, 1912.

At the end of the vacation, May returned to her room with a promise to take better care of herself.

An illustrated letter to Win Preston reveals the cheerful optimism of its author at this time.

In Bed
Holbrook House
January 26th

Darling Win Dear,

Your long letter was a great pleasure—it was quite the longest you've ever sent me and when quite a 'bonza' one from Mabel arrived I found my cup running over! It has been such a blessing all my life to realise that the unexpected always happens—as I greatly love a surprise it has helped to pass the time along—looking out for the next—I comfort myself now that it *may* snow yet— . . . or a Publisher may take a fancy to my own style of work before I die—I might even find a good, clean man to love me—I might—have 2 babies of my own—I might find an interesting novel to read or perhaps meet a congenial soul to find a set of circumstances which provided me with some music—speaking of music—We hired a fiddle from the corner shop where the old chap is noted for his performance on the Organ with the gramophone accompaniment—the maid went in to transact the business and she returned—fiddle in one hand and bow in the other—I tuned up and Miss Parrod and I were quite happy for an hour or so—at least *I* was—I was quite surprised when the gong sounded for dinner. Somehow things were wrong at dinner—everyone was quiet. Ate little and the 2 maids were more foolish than usual and I heard something suspiciously like quarrelling in the kitchen as I went upstairs—all retired early complaining of various ills in various parts of themselves—I was disappointed as I'd hoped to give them a treat as the result of our afternoon's practice—to give a tragic note to my discomfiture I tumbled upstairs *with* the fiddle and broke the E string peg and dislodged the bridge. When the small hours of the morning were reached—the tips of my left hand fingers grew less painful and I dropped into a restless slumber—I have been reading Stanley's 'Darkest Africa'—I find it consoling to read pages and chapters and volumes of the heart rending sufferings and isolation of those poor men—my own position becomes Heavenly almost ...

For a while May honoured her promise to take better care of herself, then the pressure to finish the second history book began to take its toll and undo all the care she had been given.

The Rogers family felt an obligation to keep May's parents informed of her erratic health but, as correspondence between Europe and Australia was only as fast as the ships of the day, the news was invariably out of date, so that she was recovered when they were worried about her worsened condition and ill again when they were rejoicing in her recovery. But finally the reports from the Rogers backed up by those from Win Preston reached home with their worrying news and it was decided that, for the sake of her health, May should return to Australia. May tried desperately to fend off any plan for her return as, to her, this would signal failure. Among the preliminary sketches for *The Struggle with the Crown* were a series of notes she wrote to herself during this unsettled period.

Letters come at the wrong time.

Keep cool.

Keep your face to the sun.

Alas, my poor mother!

But her 'poor mother' took positive action and arrived unexpectedly in London to escort her daughter back to Perth. Naturally, her arrival was not welcomed by May who, at thirty-five, felt she was old enough to live her own life. The arguments became heated and, as both mother and daughter were similarly strong-willed, they eventually became bitter.

Fortunately for the Gibbs family, Win Preston intervened with a compromise. After consulting her numerous friends and contacts she suggested that the place for May to pursue her career was back in Australia but in Sydney, not Perth.

The prospect of another chance to succeed in her career was certainly attractive to May but she was still reluctant to leave London and especially her new-found friend, Rene. Doubtless her mother did not approve of the English girl—her socialist politics and radical ideas would have been abhorrent to Cecie—but, in her anxiety to get her daughter back to the sunshine of Australia, she finally proposed that Rene should accompany them. Left with no further objections, May accepted the arrangements.

With characteristic speed, once a decision had been made, Cecie delivered May's finished work to George Harrap, collected her fee and originals from her agent, packed their cases, said their farewells to the Rogers clan and the trio sailed for Australia early in 1913.

The sea voyage was again beneficial and just what May needed to make a full recovery. After a couple of weeks, she was enjoying herself. She became very friendly with one of the passengers, a Captain Richard Crawshay of the Dragoons, who was retiring from India. He was a powerful looking man with striking good looks, and came to the rescue of a group of passengers, which included May, when some hooligans played up on the ship.

> The Captain, an immaculately dressed Englishman, went in with both fists and, much to everyone's delight, knocked the offenders out.

The rest of the sea voyage, she and the captain spent a great deal of time in one another's company and he confided in her his plans to buy a property in Australia. Before the journey ended he had proposed to her but May's views of marriage had not changed and she could not see herself in the role of a farmer's wife. Their friendship was to continue by spasmodic letter writing, mostly from the captain. She received his last letter many months later.

> I had a pencilled short letter from Flanders just before the word 'Go!' He talked of the terrible mud and his pride in being given his command of the cavalry.
>
> I was so moved that he should remember me at such a time.

A hero of the First World War, Richard Crawshay was killed with his men not long after this note was written.

May and Rene left the ship at Perth and spent a few weeks at The Dune, during which time May re-established contact with the *Western Mail* and began a series of satirical cartoons for them. Quite soon, however, the clash of personalities between May's mother and her English friend became pronounced and the two women headed for the east coast as had been agreed.

On arrival in Sydney, May and Rene took rooms at one of the numerous boarding houses clinging to the edge of Ben Boyd Road, Neutral Bay. The location was ideal, near the city, but separated from the bustle of the commercial world by the broad harbour. Sydney was not London but it was far more exciting than Perth and it was certainly the publishing centre of Australia. Although not a giant industry, publishing was a thriving one for professional illustrators. Isolated from the rest of the world, publishers were forced to rely on local talent and experienced illustrators could earn good money.

Almost from the day she arrived in Sydney, May's career was on the ascent. The Australian publishing firm Angus and Robertson was to give her her first job illustrating the cover of Eleanor Mack's novel, *Scribbling Sue.* The project was a delight for her as the central character of the novel had a lot in common with her own 'Mimie' of *Mimie and Wog.*

Frank Fox, editor of the *Lone Hand,* a popular Australian magazine of the day, commissioned her to draw the black swan of Western Australia for an issue and this was to be followed by the most substantial contract she had ever received.

The *Sydney Mail,* then a major New South Wales newspaper, carried a feature front page and the editor, W. R. Charlton, gave her a trial cover to complete. She passed the test and the initial order was followed with a request for twenty-five original covers.

This was the most challenging assignment she had undertaken and she was determined the covers would be striking.

> I used to do anything that came in my mind that made an effective cover. Most often I think a fancy idea, a face with it. It had to be something striking and I used to make a striking effect. I think I always did.

They were highly successful, and, as was the custom of the day, some became collector's items. May Gibbs' character study to illustrate a popular short story, *The Mate of the Wakarool*, is a particularly arresting work.

Although May lived at Neutral Bay, she worked in the city, at No. 4 Bridge Street, high up in a room she called the 'Little Studio' and she grew to love the daily ferry trips to the city.

Sunny Sydney was in marked contrast to foggy London so although she was back into the routine of hard work and meeting deadlines her health was unaffected. It was, moreover, stimulating and her productivity steadily grew, fired by praise from her publishers.

The principal of the Sydney Teachers' College, Percival R. Cole, wrote an article for the *Sunday Mail*, titled 'Social Life in a Sydney School', which was illustrated by May Gibbs. As a result Mr Cole became an admirer of her work and their friendship lasted a lifetime. This initial contact also resulted in May's illustrating for the New South Wales Education Department and generations of school children became familiar with her drawings in the *Primary Reader*. Articles and accompanying pictures were to appear in the *School Magazine* for some fifty years, which made May the most published contributor to it.

Apart from being her most productive year to that date, 1913 was the year May Gibbs gave birth to the characters who were to immortalise her in Australian children's literature—the gumnut babies.

May in 'Little Studio', which she called the room where she worked, high up in No. 4 Bridge Street, Sydney.

8

'WE ARE THE GUMNUT CORPS'

> *Miss Gibbs has made a genuine and original contribution to our Australian folklore.*
>
> *Bulletin, Sydney 1917*

'I could almost draw before I could walk,' May was to recall. While few of her youthful drawings remain, in the body of the work she had produced by her late thirties there is evidence of most of the elements found in her best-loved creations—her ability for acute observation, her whimsical humour and her penchant and talent for figure work. There are youthful drawings of naked children, the chubby cupid theme developed in her teens, and finally her work with child models at the Mary Woodward Little Studios. It required one final ingredient stirred on by an active imagination to produce the bush babies.

On her return to Australia and move to Sydney, May had quickly discovered the Blue Mountains bushland. While not quite as exuberant as her native Western Australian heath, the plants of the sandstone escarpments were not entirely alien. There were gum trees bearing flower and nut, fluffy wattles, boronias and some new finds—flannel flowers, grey spiders of grevillea, Christmas bells. There were also banksias bearing their shaggy load.

> It's hard to tell, hard to say, I don't know if the bush babies found me or I found the little creatures. Perhaps it was memories of West Australian wild flowers and trips to Blackheath.

Here then was inspiration, and, as her imagination began to work on it, gradually the bush fairyland began to emerge and its tiny inhabitants to make their way into May's illustrations.

Early developments of the gumnuts appeared in two separate publications in 1913. In the Christmas number of the *Sydney Mail*, 10 December 1913, May illustrated a headpiece for a children's story, *The Magic Button*, by Ethel Turner. Two pretty children, Dot and Dash, occupy one side of the page, while a grotesque gnome balances on a gumleaf and observes their interest in a magic button. Close to the gnome, barely discernible, are little characterless faces, peeping out of the gumnuts. You have to look closely, but they are there.

About this time May was also commissioned to illustrate *A Little Bush Poppy*, written by Edith Graham. One of the illustrations, which carried the caption, 'Oh so happy we were in the moonlight', shows a boy of eight years looking on in wonderment at the meeting of the fairies of the old world with the bush sprites of the southern continent. The forerunners of the gumnuts and blossom babies appear to be agreeable little characters from their very beginning.

Commissions from publishers for illustrative work and from individuals commissioning watercolour portraits ensured May a livelihood but the babies continued to kick and gradually made their way into the artist's consciousness, making their first appearance in the middle of the night. May had begun venturing into commercial areas and wanted a theme for a good Australian book mark.

> I thought of the Australian gumleaf, which was an ideal shape for a bookmark and a pretty thing. If only I could make it interesting on both sides. In the middle of the night I awoke, and, in fancy, saw peeping over a long gumleaf, a little bush sprite with a gumnut on its head. I hand painted them and Lucy Peacock of the Roycroft Library sold them for me at 5s each. They became so popular, later we printed them and sold thousands for 6d each.

Titled by a contemporary journalist 'The Spirit of the Bush', it marked the appearance of the first real gumnut baby.

Their debut in print was made soon after in J. F. Archibald's literary magazine, *Lone Hand*. On the cover of the January 1914 issue, a baker's dozen of gumnut babies peer between, over and from behind a striking cluster of gumleaves.

The *Sydney Mail* had commissioned May to do twenty-five covers and, intrigued with the little figures, W. R. Charlton, the publisher, encouraged her to include them in material submitted. Thus very shyly, the bush fairies made their appearances. The gumnut covers were followed by covers featuring wattle babies, flannel flower babies and Christmas bell babies. 'The Spirit of the Bush' prompted further works, including postcards, and, within a year, the babies had become part of the Australian culture.

In December 1914 the *Sydney Morning Herald* summed up their success.

> That she uses all Australian flower and leaf forms in her artistic work is one of the chief charms which Miss May Gibbs manages to infuse in all she does.

> This kind of work is so womanly, in the best sense, that it is a fresh proof of the deep feeling for nature, which is nourished by living in such beautiful surroundings as we enjoy in Sydney.
>
> It is in the loving and fanciful treatment, with its quaint turn of humour given to our Christmas Flowers by Miss Gibbs, that she catches the fancy of her admirers. As a woman artist 'with a way of her own', Miss Gibbs has carefully made her mark.

When the threat of war became reality and the first of the diggers left for overseas, the bush babies also signed up. May's series of cards for the armed forces, in giving pleasure to the soldiers overseas, helped establish the foundation for four generations of May Gibbs fans and drew the following accolade from the press:

> Miss Gibbs' treatment of the gum tree flowers is particularly charming and unique, and they hold pride of place as public favourite of all her rare original work.

Having established herself as an artist, May was anxious to once again turn her talents to writing and to create a book featuring the babies.

> The first Australian books I ever did were the flower books, *Gum-Nut Babies* and *Gum-Blossom Babies.* I thought to myself I'll make the pictures first and write the stories around them because the pictures will sell the book. The stories just rolled out of me, I had no trouble at all.

Angus and Robertson, the senior publishers in Australia, agreed to handle the books and their managing editor, F. S. Shenstone, settled on a royalty of $12\frac{1}{2}$ per cent of the selling price of each book.

On 5 December 1916, just in time for the Christmas market, May Gibbs' first Australian book appeared, entitled *Gum-Nut Babies.* From its cover blue gumnut baby eyes peered over perfectly shaped gumleaves and reflected astonishment at the human readers returning their gaze. As the reader turned the first page, another illustration revealed more gumleaves supporting small bodies, each fitted with a pair of tiny wings and a gumnut hat. Eleven pages of illustrations in the booklet carried captions and opposite each illustration May Gibbs made her first observations of the gumnuts' lifestyle.

Gum-Nut Babies was charmingly presented with an accompanying envelope and made a delightful Christmas gift. Priced at one shilling each, the first print run of 3000 sold out as soon as it reached the shops.

The second booklet, *Gum-Blossom Babies*, was released later but in time for the same Christmas. Though it was almost identical in length to the first bush baby book it had a greater page extent and sold for 2s 6d. Much to the author's and publisher's pleasure this book was also an immediate sell out.

The critical response to these books was quite as extraordinary.

> *Gum-Nut Babies* and *Gum-Blossom Babies* are two of the quaintest of distinctly Australian booklets that have been put on the market. It is too late in the day to expatiate on the pretty conceit and cleverness of these little studies for their popularity has long since spread over the continent. Miss May Gibbs is an institution of which we are unreservedly proud, and we want the other side of the world to know about her.
>
> The Bookman, *Sunday Times*, London, 7 October 1917

> May Gibbs has made a genuine and an original contribution to our Australian folklore. Her Gumnuts and Gum Blossom Babies deserve their wide popularity, they are as distinctive as the Kewpie . . .
>
> *Bulletin*, Sydney, November 1917

> These little creatures belong to the same category as the leprechauns of Irish fairy tales. The artist gives a quaint individuality to her little people and, if the world is not getting too materialistic, she may perhaps be laying the foundation of a new Australian folklore.
>
> *Evening News*, Sydney 1917

Encouraged by both critical acclaim and commercial success May wrote three more bush baby books which Angus and Robertson published. These were *Boronia Babies*, and *Flannel Flowers and Other Bush Babies* in 1917, and *Wattle Babies* in 1918. The popularity of the bush folk was again borne out by the sales of the books to 1920—*Gum-Nut Babies* 32,627, *Gum-Blossom Babies* 32,843, *Wattle Babies* 23,016, *Boronia Babies* 19,450, *Flannel Flowers and Other Bush Babies* 18,727. The bush babies who had made their first publishing appearance in *Lone Hand* had established themselves, as the *Evening News* had predicted, as part of Australian folklore.

9

'GETTING FAR TOO FLASH'

> *I'm looking at some most charming red and bronze tipped gumleaves which are in the green vase you gave me. I've a new spring sofa in the corner and Mabel says I'm getting far too flash. I'm just as mean as ever and Rene is just as lavish.*
>
> *Letter to Win Preston from May Gibbs in her studio*

A reporter for the Sydney *Sunday Sun* interviewed May Gibbs at her workplace and the article, as fulsome in turn of phrase as it is in praise, is nevertheless a valuable contemporary view.

> Have you ever passed by the magic bower in the midst of a work-a-day prosaic Sydney, where the Gumnut Babies first saw daylight?
>
> Take a peep in; it does your heart good in the midst of oblong, ugly, heavy world worries, and a smile will creep in and lift from your shoulders for a moment the heavy burden of actualities.
>
> Such a bright pretty studio, workmanlike, yet graced with sketches, flowers and some rare china specimens, and bending over her brush and painting is the brown headed, curly headed sprite at whose bidding the gumnut babies and wattle blossom elves and the creatures of the bush come tripping from fairyland for our delight.
>
> Miss May Gibbs has carved for herself a distinct niche in the world of Australian art, which in no way resembles the achievement of 'popular artists' who leap from obscurity to success with one lucky 'catch' stunt that may be repeated feverishly with monotony while the craze lasts, and then never are they heard of again.

It had been almost three years since May had offered her first gumnut books for publication. Life during this period was indeed good. She was rewarded with as many assignments as she could handle and she had successfully ventured into a number of commercial projects. Her name was well known throughout Australia; Miss Gibbs was something of a minor celebrity.

She discovered she quite enjoyed the recognition she was receiving. A relatively shy person, except with those very close to her, she grew to enjoy the congratulations from strangers who recognised her from newspaper articles. The compliments gave her an inner glow, though she was rather put out by one fan's comment,

'I thought you'd be much taller'. She was quite aware she 'sat tall but stood short' and found no pleasure in being reminded of it.

Her only close friends during this period were Rene, and Rachel Matthews, whom the women had befriended and who was also sharing rooms in Ben Boyd Road, Neutral Bay. Rene had obtained a position as a telephonist at the GPO in Sydney and she and May travelled together in the ferry to the city each day.

There was an extensive bohemian element in Sydney during this period. The writers and artists had established their own circle largely centred on J. F. Archibald's *Bulletin* magazine and the Society of Artists, which included such luminaries as Norman Lindsay, Sydney Ure Smith, Sydney Long and Julian Ashton. May does not appear to have been a part of any group. The artists would regularly get together for practice in live work when a suitable model would be found to pose for them, but the only life studies which appear in her work of this period are modelled by Rene. In a letter to Win Preston she revealed a little of her social reserve.

> I had an invitation to a Committee of Humorous Artists to decide upon details for a proposed Humorous Exhibition of Humorous Art— I like seeing funny people—but I didn't go—I had one of these 'can't' attitudes of mind—I'm sorry now ...

She had always prided herself on being an individual and the pattern of her life to this date showed her as fiercely independent. Certainly she now had Rene and Rachel but these relationships, while complementing her personality, left her free to get on with her career. The rather unorthodox lifestyle obviously suited the forty-year-old artist.

She had escaped from the restrictive elements of The Dune and the frequent arguments with her mother. She no longer felt obliged to vindicate her single status and seemed positively delighted that she was unmarried and therefore unhampered, with Rene and Rachel satisfying any need she may have for love. She had one of the characters for whom she was obviously the model express her views on the subject in a short story written at that time but never published.

> 'It's all wrong, parents shall understand. When I broke away mother was terrible—I'll never forget how she sat as if she were turned to stone when I kissed her goodbye—she didn't say a word, it

> nearly broke me, but I steeled myself and went through—and now, why they think far more of me than ever before—I've proved myself—made my way—achieved a little success and they're quite proud of it. I don't care what you say, L.S.D.* counts. I make my money now just like the boys and they respect me. If I'd stayed at home, what would I be, probably an irritable, snappy old maid ... I've no doubt we're all meant to be married but if you can't the next best thing is to cut away from home and make some sort of place in the world for yourself.'

But, early in 1918 May had been away from home long enough to feel she could return for a visit, knowing she could leave for the more uninhibited lifestyle of Sydney whenever she became restless. Behind her were several years of hard work, culminating in financial success and, more importantly, literary recognition.

The sea voyage from Sydney to Fremantle ensured that she was completely rested and it was a happy reunion for May and her parents. Ivan, the 'Wreck of the *Hesperus*', had enlisted and was still somewhere overseas; Harold, who had been rejected for service on health grounds, was on one of his periodic disappearances, but Cecie and Herbert were both happy and proud as they welcomed their daughter home. The Italian, Calanchini, who was still the Gibbs' permanent boarder, was also there to greet her. Still a most ardent admirer, he discussed her at great length with a fellow ferry traveller, James Ossoli Kelly. Calanchini had followed May's success with devoted interest. It was he who christened her 'The Genius'—a name she quite liked to assume on many of her postcards.

The Dune, South Perth, was much the same as May remembered it and these few weeks were some of the happiest spent with her parents. Probably because she had much more confidence in herself, she was more relaxed with them. Herbert was particularly interested in the artists of Sydney and spent hours discussing the craftsmanship of the black and white illustrators Australia was producing. There was also great discussion about the direction May's art had taken and both agreed that her new career was far more rewarding than the journalistic illustrating she had pursued in Perth. The artist's gumnut theme had snowballed into a small industry, each step leading to a new way to present the bush babies.

* Pre-decimalisation of the coinage, L.S.D. was an abbreviation of the Latin for pounds, shillings and pence.

While in Perth May received a request via Angus and Robertson from the then National Art Gallery, New South Wales, for the original watercolour used on the cover of *Gum-Blossom Babies.* Aware of her own worth by this time, she was unflattered by the request and her reply reveals, albeit lightheartedly, the businesslike approach to her work that was to make such a strong impression on all who subsequently had professional dealings with her.

The Dune

Dear Mr Shenstone,

Give the Blossom drawing to the Gallery with my love but say I don't like being represented by that little bit and will they please buy at a large fat price very soon—a large, fine masterpiece in Gumnuts that I have in my mind!!! Don't forget the message.

Yes thank you I'm having a nice holiday working harder than usual!

With kind regards
Yours sincerely
May Gibbs

It was a mentally and physically refreshed author who returned to Sydney to prepare for the publication of what was to be the most important book of her career. It had been a long and difficult 'birth'. The book is first mentioned in May's correspondence in 1917.

'Little Studio'
Queensland Offices
Bridge Street
5 June 1917

Dear Mr Shenstone,

When may I hear results of your consideration of the book 'Snugglepot and Cuddlepie'? Everything is ready and I'm just longing to get on with it—days are slipping by horribly quickly and I do want it out early!

Yours anxiously!!!
May Gibbs

My apologies for not remembering your initials.

It is not known how long it took May to write the first Snugglepot and Cuddlepie adventure, *Tales of Snugglepot and Cuddlepie,* for the story obviously draws on a lifetime of observation. However, once the book was written and with Angus and Robertson, May was understandably anxious for a decision and pursued her publishers with vigour and skilful tactics. The successful author knew her worth and could feel sure her reference to another publisher would guarantee an answer from her correspondent.

4 July 1917

Dear Mr Shenstone,

Here are the leaves, and by the way *PLEASE* have the printing of the books *good and clear* this time. I should be glad if you would allow me to see proofs while the printing is going on.

With regard to 'Snugglepot and Cuddlepie', I feel that not another moment can be spared. I may be missing all other chances by waiting so long for you—I believe I have a good introduction to Lothian in Melbourne, for whom I've already worked. I feel sure you'll understand how keen I am about keeping the ball rolling. I feel it would be bad to miss this year, so I want you to tell me definitely and quickly what you've decided. Please forgive the hustling note. I'm very fuzzy and half awake with my cold and am seized with terror at the way the months are flying. May I expect an answer from you right away?

Yours sincerely,
May Gibbs
I know it's not your fault things are slow, but you can pull the strings!

The dedication for this Australian children's classic reads 'To the Two Dearest Children in the World, Lefty and Bill'. Few readers knew that these were the author's nicknames for her mother and father.

With twenty-two full-page pictures and 10,000 words scattered with illustrations to highlight the action, *Tales of Snugglepot and Cuddlepie* was released late in 1918, and the response of the Australian public must have been gratifying to both the author and her publishers—they scooped up the first, second and third editions. Of the characters' names, May Gibbs said:

I thought of the name Snugglepot for a book on bush babies, but I could not get another name. I wanted two, and one night, lying in bed quietly, I thought of Snugglepot ... Cuddlepie!

In two sentences, the author established the personalities of the gumnut foster brothers.

'I want to see a Human,' said Snugglepot.

'In the distance,' said Cuddlepie.

Snugglepot, the leader, and the gentle Cuddlepie are influenced by the stories of an old wise kookaburra, who talks of humans: 'Strong as the Wind, swift as the River, fierce as the Sun.' Kookaburra not only instils caution in the gumnuts, but arouses the spirit of adventure in them and so 'The Journey Begins'.

The gumnuts meet up with many of the bush creatures, who respond to the goodwill and friendly efforts of the adventurers and, on the way, the storyteller draws the attention of the reader to the meticulously detailed pictures supplied with the prose, pictures which amply repay the close scrutiny and prolonged study of childhood.

Little Ragged Blossom, the frog Lanky Legs, the Red Gumnut, Lilly Pilly and assorted nuts and blossoms are featured and a lasting friendship is sustained with Mr Lizard, who pops in and out of the gumnuts' adventures in the most unlikely places.

To balance good with evil May Gibbs introduced the bad Banksia Men and Mrs Snake—formidable foes for the adventurers and their companions.

> The Banksia Men arrived in this way. When I was out walking, over in Western Australia, with my cousins, we came to a grove of banksia trees, and sitting on almost every branch were these ugly little, wicked little men that I discovered and that's how the Banksia Men were thought of.

Critics of May Gibbs' stories were most distressed about the effect the Banksia Men had on young readers, and the reaction surprised the author.

> One day I received a letter, a very angry letter, saying that it was wicked to make drawings of these Banksia Men to frighten the lives out of children. He'd torn the page out of my book where Banksia Men were on it, and scribbled it all out and dashed it with a heavy pencil, and wrote me a very nasty letter.
>
> I think getting accustomed—I mean, children getting accustomed— to ugly things like Banksia Men and that sort of thing, it strengthens them if anything, and then they find that they're not all bad, things are not so bad as they seem.

In a thoughtful resumé of May's achievement published in 1977 on the centenary of her birth, a latter-day critic concurs with May's beliefs.

> Gibbs has a firmer grasp on the grimmer realities of life for a five year old and for us over-fives, than comparable English writers such as A. A. Milne and Beatrix Potter. The dangers and nasty characters the intrepid bushbabies face emerge from darker regions of the subconscious than Milne's 'Heffalump' or the foxes and Farmer MacGregors in Beatrix Potter. The giant squid and giant octopus, dark holes and spiders, snakes and Banksia men of *The Complete Adventures of Snugglepot and Cuddlepie* focus on strangely recognisable images; the unspoken and nameless horrors of childhood. Not the least of May Gibbs' achievements is the way, however unintentionally, she releases and copes with these images from the collective unconscious of children.
>
> Bronwen Handyside, *Lip Magazine*

At the time of publication the reviewers both at home and abroad were enchanted simply by the book's novelty and its distinctly Australian flavour.

> *Tales of Snugglepot and Cuddlepie* is an Australian story about Two Little Gumnuts. It may be a little puzzling, for there are many queer creatures in it, besides those of the title; and, as they do not conform to our old nursery traditions, no doubt the grown up reader will be asked many questions. For instance, there is a weird bird called a kookaburra and a boat called a Kurrajong. The illustrations on nearly every page are lively and original and complete a fascinating story.
>
> *Spectator*, London

> This lady has a great charm for young Australians. There are artists more ambitious by far and in some ways more original who still do not get a hundredth part of Miss Gibbs' very real popularity. It is a stroke of genius on the part of the authoress to have furnished Australian 'babies' with homes, furniture, and clothing of Australian bush 'primary production'.
>
> *Australian Woman's Mirror*

> I bought a whole set of the 'Gum Nuts', 'Gum Blossom' and 'Wattle Babies', as well as 'Snugglepot and Cuddlepie', and gloriously exhibited them to a circle of acquaintances who immediately prevailed upon me to let them have the books.
>
> Miles Franklin, *Australian Products in England*

Messrs Angus and Robertson have proved themselves a much wiser Board of Health than the departments in Macquarie Street and Queen Street, and one of the best physicians in our Australian city is Miss May Gibbs.

Medical Journal of Australia

There has never been a more beautiful book published than 'Snugglepot and Cuddlepie'.

Ladies' Sphere, Perth

May Gibbs brings the breath of the bush, the stirring of gumleaves and the twittering of feathered inhabitants. One loses the reality of trains, desk and the countinghouse.

Age, Melbourne

May Gibbs—naturalist, psychologist and artist-explorer ... has mapped out a world of her own—and conquered it completely.

Advertiser, Adelaide

May had successfully made the transition from artist to author. In twelve months, 14,414 copies had been sold in Australia and 700 in England. May had received royalties of £173 13s after five months and £383 10s after twelve months but she had had to fight for what she believed were her rights regarding royalties. And the fight is a further revelation of the astute businesswoman she was becoming.

May received a 12½ per cent royalty on the first two bush baby books, and, while she received the conventional 10 per cent royalty on *Boronia Babies* and *Wattle Babies*, she believed a 12½ per cent royalty had been established. She was therefore unprepared to accept the offered 10 per cent on *Snugglepot and Cuddlepie*. Possibly as a result of this the contract for *Snugglepot* was not signed until almost a year after publication and then only after an adamant stand by its author.

My point is simply this—if 12½% was offered to me on my first assignment—and because I hate bargaining as much as you do—I am absolutely determined I want 12½% on S & C ...

Yours sincerely M. G.

P.S. With emotion FINIS.

Please do not ask me to discuss this matter.

Angus and Robertson replied:

So be it. Please send back the S & C agreement and we shall alter it.

From 1918 to the present day, *Tales of Snugglepot and Cuddlepie* has virtually never been out of print. In addition to the original book, a small paperback was published in 1929. The prose was practically unabridged but it only carried four full-page illustrations and was titled *Snugglepot and Cuddlepie — Their Adventures Wonderful.*

A wartime edition was printed in 1940, titled *The Complete Adventures of Snugglepot and Cuddlepie.* It combined the three gumnut books, *Tales of Snugglepot and Cuddlepie, Little Ragged Blossom* and *Little Obelia,* and a number of full-page illustrations were eliminated.

From 1946 to 1950, the book was enlarged to accommodate more of the May Gibbs full-page illustrations and the publishers once again expanded the book in 1968 to include the colour plates. This version, which features a blue cover, is still in print and, together with a paperback issue in 1984, is the only 'Snugglepot and Cuddlepie' edition which carries May Gibbs' original drawings. Other editions have been redrawn and edited and in the process, many believe, have lost the May Gibbs quality and charm.

The bride in Northam, Western Australia, in 1919.

The groom, James Ossoli Kelly. Years later May admitted of this Irish gentleman. 'The day I first met J.O., I thought, "There's the man I'm going to marry!"'

10

MARRIED

I've not given you the autographed Snug and Cud, and I did not write the nice letter to Mr Robertson that I intended to — but I got married! It needs no further explanation or excuse, does it?

Letter to Angus and Robertson

On 11 November 1918, the armistice proclaiming the end of the First World War was signed, beside which joyful event, May wrote, the publication of her 'little book' some weeks earlier, had paled in importance. Yet another event, which was to become significant, had claimed a share of her attention in this crowded year. While visiting her parents that year she had met Calanchini's friend and ferry companion James Ossoli Kelly.

Some months before May's visit the gracious Calanchini had invited the lonely Irishman to meet Cecie and Herbert. Herbert had been impressed by his practical knowledge of the mining industry while Cecie was charmed by his manners, obvious schooling, and impeccable dress sense. His interest in the arts also made him welcome in the Gibbs' household and among their circle of friends. 'Met the Gibbs family through medium of Calanchini' J. O., as he was known to all his friends, had recorded in his diary, and, after further meetings, Herbert was to write to his daughter saying he had met the man she should marry.

When May visited soon after, Cecie may have hoped for a match between her daughter and the obviously devoted Calanchini, but it became increasingly clear to all that, while yet evincing her independent stance, May was somewhat intrigued by the cultured and socially assured Irishman. When May left soon after for Sydney, she was presumably no nearer the state of matrimony that both her parents would have welcomed for her. However, she kept in touch with this interesting new friend and he with her.

Sydney
Wednesday, November 1918

Dear Kelly, James and Ossoli,

This will be an attempt to write to you. These days are days of intense feeling—days of vague soul stirrings—for me at least—I am swept off my mind's feet—it is all so terribly moving. After our first Burst of Joy on Friday morning we settled into steady, tense anxious waiting—then when the news came at last we were wildly joyous again and since then it has been queer mixed feelings that have passed our storm swept souls—the Joy of it all but the tears for all it has meant.

This is not the first letter I've started for you, but the excitement has been too much. Then, as a result of all my overwork during the last few months I've been enduring a kind of neuritis in my head that made all thinking efforts beyond me.

My little book is out—I was excited about it, once—ages ago in the early days of November 1918. It is now as if I had never slaved for it, worried over it, shed tears because of it. Nothing matters—The War is Over—Try as I will I can't realise that as I want to—it numbs me—I feel heavy and stupid—my little soul is overpowered and so nature protects in times of great emotional stress ...

No I did not meet Mrs Pigeon and I'm truly sorry that I saw so little of Miss Bullivant. It was a bad time for us to meet. She being under such a Cloud and I with my work sapping every bit of energy.

You think me a sad Money Grubber—A woman losing her Cast in Business Affairs—Yes? You think I no longer take an interest in Social Things. I am losing touch with People who might easily help me to be myself more successfully? Maybe, but to be frank—I was born without a taste for Social things—Society People do not appeal to me—I hate being in the Company of more than one or two people at one time.

Two Days Later—This is a most silly letter. Somehow I've lost all confidence in myself as a correspondent. I have a feeling, as I get older, that I have no power to express myself—to begin with—I hardly know my own mind—I find I have few steady convictions—no settled opinions—and I want less and less to talk about myself.

This morning I had set aside to write letters and there have been such hopeless interruptions and there goes the Luncheon bell! ...

What you say about my work is true—I can do better but one must take the opportunity when it offers—I have taken mine but I'm not unmindful of its dangers—you said some very nice things about me—I like it I do like them—but you are such a dear optimist and you have the dearest way of seeing the best in everyone. It is perhaps the best gift nature can bestow upon a ____. It will be a great disap-pointment to me if you turn out to be less—less—well anything less than—than you really are. But you know dear person, one could never be quite certain—it's the last thing I should like to suggest on any unthinking mind but you know of a certainty as well as I do that people are mostly disappointing—I would say to all girls and women—find some work and make that your Happiness in life—get all the love and joy and fun you can from People but do not *depend* upon Humans for ——.

Imagine me in a state of merriment just here—this, dear Ossoli, is how I talk when the thermometer rises—I mean barometer—Oh! goodness!! it's just like being in a tightly shut bathroom with hot water running and no outlet for the steam.

Someday I'll read all those books you've told me of—I've kept your letters with them in—I have not your last letter here so I can't answer it—by the way I've meant to send back your Play and keep forgetting.

I had a letter from Home about you—a letter from Teddy about you and one from Mother with news of you all by one mail—a few weeks ago.

On second thoughts I'm not sending you a copy of 'Snugglepot and Cuddlepie', the poor little chaps would feel uncomfortable in the atmosphere of your Classics. Your fine old friends would be offended at the intrusion and my babies would be terribly unloved.

I promised one to Miss Bullivant so I'm sending one but they won't be happy there either—but they'll fare better there than with you.

I am sitting by a window overlooking the Bay—it is veiled with a blue mist—in spite—of the strong wind that's blowing. Ferries and little sailing boats are passing—it's very Charming. For rest and peace of mind—for real pleasure—one turns to Nature. There's a lovely Poplar not far from my bedroom window—it is a perfect song of Peace and Consolation to me when I feel tired in heart and mind.

Yes I love Portraiture—and if I had been one scrap less rushed when your dear Friend was here I should have asked her to sit for me for I believe I could have made a sketch of her that would have pleased you.

I'd just love to say a teasing thing to you!!! I'm dying to. I love teasing some people and you are very nice to tease but I won't—

Here is my hand in a warm grasp because of the Great Victory.

Yours very sincerely
Cecilia

It is not known how much this friendship was responsible for May's decision to return to Perth for Christmas 1918—her second visit in twelve months. Certainly she had other excuses, a busy and successful year and the 'Great Victory' to celebrate with the family, the need of a rest. It was certainly in cheerful voice that she excused herself to her publishers though the skittish mood of her opening does not inhibit her concern for her work and the perfection of its presentation.

> The Dune
> December 2, 3, or 4
> Hullo! Shenny—*I mean*
>
> Dear Mr Shenstone,
>
> Good morning! Are you too busy to see me? For a moment! May I go over to the west for a holiday! There's nothing to see to is there—only if there should be another Edition while I'm away you'll have those little things seen to that we discussed won't you?
>
> As far as I can remember they were—
> 1 Snugglepot (*and*) Cuddlepie the 'and' is too large it would improve the look of cover—also in the beginning at head of first page.
> 2 Frontispiece—lettering too close to drawing
>
> There may be other points. I thought there were quite a number but I forget and it's close to mail time.
>
> I suppose nothing can be done to lighten the extreme blackness of the 'Diving Pool' and 'Second hand houses'.
>
> Rene tells me in the letter I had from her this morning that you are doing well with them. (I sincerely hope you'll forgive me for going off without coming to see if there was anything to be done. I'm just recovering from a long journey and a cold.)
>
> I hope you are very well
>
> Yours sincerely
>
> May Gibbs
>
> I had a lovely present of *white onions*!!! yesterday.

Christmas 1918 saw the return of many of the servicemen from the war in Europe and, with them, a most virulent strain of influenza which quickly spread and took a tremendous toll of the east coast population. Because of May's bronchial weakness, Rene and Rachel persuaded her to stay in the West. Her work was shipped to Western Australia. To Herbert's pleasure his daughter took over his studio and settled down to work in Perth for a couple of months. It was uncharacteristic of May to concede so readily. She had always shown a complete disregard for her health and yet she changed her plans so willingly and decided to stay in Perth. The reason was now undoubtedly James Ossoli Kelly.

Who was this stranger who had engaged the affections of the independent and choosy Miss Gibbs?

His father was army, Colonel Kelly of the Wiltshires, so it was natural for James and his brother Oliver to attend Stonyhurst College, well known for its military regime, and then Clongoweswood College, Ireland. Their mother died in 1881, when the boys were at Stonyhurst, and on his grandfather's death in 1885, J. O. left Clongoweswood and worked at the National Bank of Ireland, Charing Cross, London.

In 1889, he joined the wave of migrants to Australia and, on 14 November, landed in Melbourne after a lengthy sea voyage on the P. & O. ship, *Carthage*.

His first venture was a rented farm at Stonyford in the Western District of Victoria and it was here that Oliver joined him. J. O.'s attempt at farming was a failure and, with what little money he could muster, he headed for the Coolgardie goldfields during the 1896 gold rush, while Oliver decided to try his luck in the eastern states.

Unfortunately, J. O. fared no better prospecting and, with the rest of the luckless men, vied for the 'positions vacant' on the company mines. A six-month stint underground was his real apprenticeship to mining, after which he moved on to running cyanide plants and assaying at company mines with flamboyant investor-tempting names like 'Duke' and 'Lady Bountiful'.

Along with his brother, J. O. volunteered for the Boer War but he was rejected while Oliver was accepted and sailed for South Africa. During 1900, he again tried for the army, but the third and fourth Western Australian contingents left Australian shores without him.

During the next decade, he became part of a migratory mining population, moving from outpost to outpost as work became available. Accumulated pay was usually dissipated in a splurge on the bright lights of Melbourne or another prospecting venture which always ended in a negative result.

When the Boer War ended, Oliver elected to stay on in South Africa and, in direct contrast to J. O.'s Australian experience, was to achieve some success in Rhodesia (now Zimbabwe).

By 1914, when J. O. was again rejected for military service, Oliver convinced him to visit Africa, and for four years he enjoyed the white man's lifestyle in southern Rhodesia.

> A pleasant life, shooting trips with a walk through the Makaha Valley, nigger servants, pleasant neighbours and an attempt to a claim with no good results.

Although the brothers and a partner won some £12,000 worth of gold from a claim, malaria, pneumonia and typhoid all took their toll on J. O.'s health and his journal records the adverse turn in their fortunes.

> East Coast fever stopped our transport and prices of cyanide (£24 a ton) and mercury (£40 a flask) knocked us out. A year's hard work, none of us fit, costs mounting dreadfully and ore very refractory.

In 1917 J. O. decided to return to Australia with a friend, Neil Irvine. He motored from Makaha to Salisbury (now Harare) and, after a wait in Durban, boarded the *Ascanius*. He spent a few days in Melbourne but the West still beckoned and he headed back to Perth.

After the years in Africa, attended by servants, the crude conditions of the Australian goldfields had little appeal for the educated Irishman and he sought a job with the government wheat scheme which offered security with a regular salary. A public servant in a routine office job, he showed some semblance of settling down by moving from the hotel where he had temporary residence to a permanent room in South Perth.

This was the man who, for months, sympathetically listened to Calanchini's tale of unrequited love and, on meeting Miss Gibbs, promptly proceeded to woo her himself. The importance of their first meeting is recorded in his diary which states, in large, bold writing, 'Today I Met Miss Gibbs'.

May does not appear to have recorded the event in diary or notebook but, years later, she admitted, 'The day I first met J. O., I thought, "There's the man I'm going to marry!" '

What attracted May to the Irishman? He was well mannered, beautifully spoken and intelligent, but so were most of the gentlemen she had been meeting at her parents' home for twenty years.

He was presentable but could only be considered reasonably good looking. With his public service job, with limited prospects, he was hardly a worthwhile catch for a woman who was now earning more than most of her male friends. At forty-two she could have felt the need for companionship but this is unlikely because this was surely provided by Rene and Rachel who were warm and loving friends of many years.

J. O. was not exactly free when he decided to court May. For almost twenty years he had had a close relationship with a wealthy Melbourne socialite. Their affair was drawing to a rather happy conclusion—he had, somewhat reluctantly, agreed to marry her and they were considered engaged by their friends—when J. O. met May Gibbs. There is no record of the fiancée's reaction to the sudden change of plans. May remembered:

> He lived away at the ends of the earth on the Goldfields but put his blacks into a trunk and spent his holidays in Melbourne where much social doings with his friend (never fiancée) was a BIG UN. Well, he always came back still unengaged. At least it was announced to all in the best circles they were engaged, then I came into the picture, all innocent and very interested. His Mines Boss who told me the story loved him and could not understand why he didn't marry her.

Their initial meeting was quickly followed up with a hastily written note, 'Will you meet me for lunch?', which the Irish gentleman slipped into her hand.

Uncharacteristically, May is reported to have behaved like a teenager during the courtship. Marjorie Ridley, a second cousin who was much younger than May and who idolised her famous cousin, was deeply hurt when the seat she always occupied next to her was suddenly reserved for Mr Kelly. It took some time for the teenager to realise that this middleaged couple were in love.

Having waited so long to find each other, they wasted no time in announcing their intention of marrying and at Easter in 1919 they were married quietly at a registry office in Perth.

The wedding of 'The Mother of the Gumnuts' did not go unnoticed by the press.

> Quite lately in Perth, a curious phenomenon was observed. Just above roof level a cloud of diaphanous insects was seen all hurrying in the same direction. One dropped exhausted out of the throng to

lie, golden-brown and gasping on the pavement. He was a gumnut baby, curvy and fat and wreathed and capped in orange blossom.

To anxious questions he replied nothing; jumping into a taxi, he sped away to join the cloud of his brothers and sisters. They hovered in a song around her head, while May Gibbs was being made Mrs James Ossoli Kelly. When the ceremony was over they flew back, still singing into the bush. The marriage was celebrated quietly on Thursday.

Ladies' Sphere, Perth

J. O. and May spent their honeymoon at Northam, where the couple got off to a comically confused start when she absentmindedly signed the hotel register May Gibbs.

'The Dune'
South Perth, W.A.
13 May 1919

Dear Mr Shenstone,

Thank you for your good wishes so nicely expressed. I enclose the receipt for the cheque you sent me.

It's most trying being kept over here all this time and I'm hoping to be in Sydney any day now. The Boronia booklet is well on and I'm getting soaked in Fish ideas. I'm tremendously interested in the latter as you know and I wanted it to be the very best *we've* produced yet.

I've not given you the autographed Snug & Cud and I did not write the nice letter to Mr Robertson that I intended to—but I got married! It needs no further explanation or excuse, does it?

I hope you and Mr Robertson won't think my work will suffer or that the books won't be in time and all that sort of thing. My husband is an intensely booky man and helps me. I look forward to your meeting him and his meeting you—I might give an Onion Lunch in the Little Studio!

I ache to be back in my own quarters—

I hope this is a satisfactory business letter! But surely I may take a few liberties when I write to the kind guardian of Snugglepot and Cuddlepie. My husband will save you the trouble of correcting my spelling and grammer!!!! Something to be glad for?

My very best good wishes to you and Mr Robertson till we meet.

Yours very sincerely,
Cecilia May Ossoli Kelly

May Gibbs
(I like my own name best.)

May and J. O. with Rachel Matthews, a close friend who also shared rooms in Ben Boyd Road, Neutral Bay.

Rene, left, and May on the Blackheath property in 1919.

The mother of the gumnuts at work, 1920.

There was no question of settling down to married life in Perth. In fact, at no time could anyone envisage May Gibbs settling down to the role of a dutiful wife. Her career had just begun and her publishers were calling for more of her work.

The Dune
19 January, 1919

Dear Mr Shenstone,

Thank you for your wire …

PS Imagine 'Snug' and 'Cud' finding the sweetest little baby mermaid getting swallowed by a fish—hiding in shells—riding strange fish and all that sort of thing—the humour would best be made by having funny people as fish—I'm awfully *keen* on it so do get enthusiastic and make Mr Robertson like it too—*MG*

Of course I'm not certain about making 'Snug' and 'Cud' the heroes—but it rather appeals—but I'm *thinking.*

By the way I've had a few other ideas if this likes *him* not at all. Not that he *ought* to choose you know.

It took little persuasion for J. O. to give up his job at the Wheat Scheme Office to become May's manager, and the family was confident that they had found someone to look after May's business affairs while she concentrated on her career.

The newly-weds left Perth in June 1919 and travelled via the Trans-Continental Railway to Sydney.

11

FURTHER ADVENTURES

Please hurry up with the next book because we want to know what happens to the ragged blossom.

Letter to George Robertson from his granddaughter

The Kellys took rooms at Rothesay, Neutral Bay, where May had spent some time when she first arrived in Sydney. Within a day it was business as usual for May and she was off to the 'Little Studio' in Bridge Street where she settled back into work.

J. O. took charge of his creative wife's business affairs and endeavoured to learn the intricacies of the publishing world. Although she could be a stubborn negotiator when she had to be, May particularly disliked the business side of her career and was quite happy to let her husband become her business manager.

The acquisition of a husband appeared to make scant difference to May's home lifestyle and, in fact, their private married life was to be short-lived. After only six weeks, she decided the hotel was too expensive and they moved into a flat at Runnymede, Kurraba Road, Neutral Bay, where, in addition to her newly acquired husband, May insisted Rene and Rachel share the flat.

It must surely have been a strange arrangement for a man to share his bride of less than two months with two of her friends, particularly females with such strong personalities as Rene and Rachel, but J. O. appears to have accepted the situation and with equanimity christened the ménage 'May Gibbs and Associates'.

Angus and Robertson were naturally anxious for May Gibbs' next book and, with sales of her works totalling tens of thousands of copies, readily agreed to a 12½ per cent royalty.

The book, *Little Ragged Blossom and More About Snugglepot and Cuddlepie*, was published in 1920 to much critical acclaim.

> When Miss May Gibbs presented us with that quaint prose epic, *Snugglepot and Cuddlepie*, some twelve months ago, we welcomed her as a great physician, who drove dull care away. She has increased her eminence as a dissipator of gloom by the production of a sequel to that little work. Miss May Gibbs is ostensibly a Christmas treat for the young folk, but even old fogies would need to be very sour and crusty not to admit that they enjoyed every word of it.

Apart from her charming humour and style, Miss Gibbs is a naturalist of class. She knows every leaf and twig of the Australian bush and judging from her knowledge of sea cornets, anchovies, anemones and the like, she would seem to have spent at least half her life down in the mysterious deep.

The whimsical illustrations compete for supremacy with the text.

Some of them are in colour, but all of them bring a sparkle of merriment into the eye and a chuckle into the throat. We wish this delightful little volume a happy voyage into every Australian home.

Medical Journal of Australia

Miss May Gibbs has brought out another of her exceedingly clever fairy books, charming alike in the conception of its weird stories and its adaptation of Australian bird, animal and plant life to her purposes of amusing and instructing young ... numerous drawings of a quite unconventional description ...

For a greater proportion of this conception, the authoress has sought inspiration amongst fishes and seaweed. A vein of humour runs through the letter press as well as the illustrations, many of the latter being extremely amusing in a quite original fashion. The strike procession of the Nuts is clever, and at the same time not ill-natured; whilst the explanation by Winky concerning the strike as a new way of making money, will bring a smile to the staunchest unionist. 'Everyone strikes in Big Bad,' says Winky and he continues, 'The one who hits the hardest gets the most.' 'Bully ant!' exclaims Snugglepot, 'and who gets hit?' 'Everyone,' says Winky. 'Let's go away then,' said Ragged Blossom and they went.

Untitled Review

Little Ragged Blossom was also a success with its junior audience as is revealed in the following letter to George Robertson, a founder and head of the publishing division at Angus and Robertson.

Dear Jorko [George Robertson],

I like my book very much. I read it last night and love it. Do you know the story?

I like the part where the Little Ragged Blossom gets her little baby called Obelia, so that is why I panted [sic] her. Nurse said to tell you she loves her book ...

Please hurry up with the next book because we want to know what happens to the ragged blossom. She got left under the sea. Goog buy [sic]

love from Margaret

George Robertson sent the letter to May Gibbs with a note:

> The enclosed is from my grand-daughter, Marko, aged 8, and is the best 'review' we are likely to get. Congratulate yourself on her youth.

He went on to point out that the 'panting' was so good that in a few years Miss Gibbs would have to look to her laurels.

The Christmas sales for *Little Ragged Blossom and More About Snugglepot and Cuddlepie* totalled 10,338. Like *Tales of Snugglepot and Cuddlepie,* it was supported by detailed illustrations. There were two coloured plates titled 'The Society of Gumnut Artists' and 'Riding Home on the Dragons' and twenty black and white plates.

It is interesting that, for this new book, she drew on her childhood experiences and on two books she had experimented with as early as 1906, *John Dory, His Story* and *Mimie and Wog in Fishland.*

As with all her stories, she was successful in running parallel plots, sending Snugglepot and Cuddlepie off on separate adventures, then reuniting them again. She left her young readers with the unanswered question of 'What happened to ...?', assuring the multitude of readers that her next book was to be released Christmas 1921.

Sales of *Little Ragged Blossom,* at five shillings per copy, kept up steadily until the Second World War, when it was included in the *Snugglepot and Cuddlepie* omnibus, already detailed. In 1929 a smaller paperback edition of *Little Ragged Blossom* was selling for one shilling. The prose was practically untouched, though the illustrations were reduced to a handful.

The release of *Little Ragged Blossom* also helped to increase the popularity of the earlier publications.

Apart from her books May was approached by many charitable organisations for posters and one of the most effective she was to produce was for the Royal Society for the Welfare of Mothers and Babies, for which she refused payment. The poster features Dr Stork who expresses his concern to Mrs Kookaburra regarding the brand new infants he is delivering:

> I hardly like delivering the Goods, Mrs Kookaburra, them Humans is so gum careless of 'em.

For decades the picture was to grace the cover of a book produced by the New South Wales Department of Public Health on maternal and baby welfare and also act as a poster to direct young mothers to established clinics. Lady Davidson, wife of the New South Wales Governor at this time, requested the original, which was duly presented to her.

Always exploring new outlets, May decided to experiment with a new form, the yearly calendar. It was the age before the decorated calendar became the big business it is today and this enabled innovators to establish a local product and market. Edwards Dunlop of Sydney and Osboldstone and Company of Melbourne accepted her submissions to supply calendars featuring all the bush creatures, the favourite being a kookaburra depicted as a world war veteran wearing the Australian slouch hat. May and J. O. looked after the sales and distribution of the calendars and in the 1930s also took over distribution of the postcards.

May was always to have a keen eye for commercial possibilities and throughout her life had ideas for a wide range of products beyond books, postcards and calendars. She designed handkerchiefs and babies' bootees and her notebooks testify to further invention—'nice red bottle brush tea cosy', 'woolly wattle hot water bottle', 'wattle earmuffs'. 'Under the circumditions', she scribbled as preface to some short story plot ideas, 'commercialise your spare time'. Neither the short stories nor many of the inventions were to contribute to the coffers of their creator. However, some were, and badges, dolls, fabric and pottery were licensed, all displaying May's unique vision of the Australian bush.

A new book, *Little Obelia and Further Adventures of Ragged Blossom, Snugglepot and Cuddlepie*, published in 1921, was to be the third and final adventure of the original gumnut characters.

Cuddlepie makes the journey under the sea to find and rescue Ragged Blossom, while Snugglepot lives out his particular adventure with Mr Lizard.

Little Obelia boasted two colour plates. These were 'At the Races' and 'The Picture Gallery', and the remaining nineteen full-page plates were in sepia.

This story was also to be released in paperback in 1929 and in 1940 the full story was to be included in *The Complete Adventures of Snugglepot and Cuddlepie.*

Little Obelia was again supported by the critics:

> ... they are full of imagination, and are clever, bright and entertaining, to young and old alike.
>
> *Catholic Press*

> ... The illustrations show remarkable ingenuity on the part of the artist, who has given a personality to a number of familiar Australian plants and animals ... and all the grumpy grown-ups will enjoy them too.
>
> *Sydney Mail*

May had appointed her Angus and Robertson mentor, Fred Shenstone, 'Guardian' of the gumnuts, an office he was proud to accept.

> 'Shenny' presents his humble duty to the Mother of Snugglepot and Cuddlepie, and accepts the honourable office of guardian of the young gentry and their friends with a deep sense of the responsibility attaching hereto.
>
> He values highly the medium by which the notification of his appointment has been conveyed, and will ever treasure it as a token of sincere goodwill.

However, the honour of this appointment in no way intruded when a business transaction was under way.

It was with the negotiation of royalties for both *Little Obelia* and *Flannel Flowers and Other Bush Babies* that good relations with Angus and Robertson started to deteriorate. May believed she had now proved her worth and that the royalty for each should be raised to 15 per cent.

It is a tribute to May's grit in business negotiation that she won her case. Her publishers were used to paying the customary 10 per cent to such leading figures in Australian writing as Henry Lawson, 'Banjo' Paterson, C. J. Dennis and Norman Lindsay—writers whose popular appeal was every bit as persuasive a bargaining point as May's selling power.

However, possibly unaware of the experience of others, May felt she was being unfairly treated. She disliked the hard negotiation and was troubled by having to stand up for what she considered were her rights. It was the beginning of the sweet and sour relationship with Angus and Robertson that was to last her lifetime.

She must have been somewhat disappointed also at the lack of support she was receiving from her manager—husband. J. O. proved incapable of handling the hard bargaining May employed when dealing with her publishers. He stood by helplessly, while still admiring the intensity and determination his wife displayed when fighting for what she considered were her just rewards. It was the strong will that had been hinted at in the family circle. Leaving his 'little woman' to do the fighting, J. O. buried himself amongst the less volatile business of receipts and bank accounts—and the relative calm of the law courts when a gentleman was discovered illegally reproducing the babies. Action was taken and the offender was ordered to part with forty pounds' compensation for trying to capitalise on May Gibbs' creations.

When J. O. totted up the returns for the first twelve months of *Little Obelia* sales, he found they amounted to 9728 copies. Other figures he recorded were the total to that date, December 1922, of the other two titles. *Tales of Snugglepot and Cuddlepie* had sold 23,014 copies and *Little Ragged Blossom* 19,668. The latest publication showed every indication of being as successful. Thus it was to the surprise of her publishers that May did not approach them with a book for that Christmas. She appeared to be concentrating on other matters—negotiating with a Mr J. F. Wells and a Miss Vernon for Snugglepot and Cuddlepie to appear on the motion picture screen and experimenting in watercolour with the baby creatures she saw in garden flowers, which were presenting themselves as an untapped source of ideas.

The negotiations for the movie came to nothing, but two delightful characters, 'Sweet Pea' and 'Delphinium', blossomed and moved into the merchandising field. They were also the forerunners of a book May was to write some thirty years later, *Prince Dande Lion.*

In March 1921, May had been invited to exhibit at the Society of Women Painters' Exhibition at the Education Gallery in Loftus Street. She headed her list of watercolour entries with a strong portrait study of J. O. which she admitted to painting in a one-day sitting on 30 March for hanging on 1 April.

Comments from papers of the day were very guarded:

> ... and May Gibbs has caught a good deal of character.
>
> *Sunday Evening News*

> Miss May Gibbs heads her list with a strong study.
>
> *Daily Telegraph,* Sydney

> A hundred years hence they will call it a Mad Technique period. Technique first, and the truths of tone, form and colour anywhere ... so we have such pictures as Miss May Gibbs' 'Stooping Model' No. 51. No normal eye could resolve the background into a wall or anything else but a shower of brush marks which the stooping lady appears to be making an effort to dodge.
>
> *Bulletin*

May was undoubtedly disappointed by the reviews but a year later, with encouragement from her father who was staying with the Kellys in Sydney, she approached again her more serious work of portrait painting and concentrated on submissions to the Women Painters' Exhibition of that year. But again, her entries were to draw only polite comment in the newspapers.

> ... The watercolours, however, with one or two exceptions, are rather weak. Miss May Gibbs' unfinished portrait studies are interesting, and considering the difficulty of painting portraits in this medium, exceedingly creditable.
>
> *Sunday Times,* Sydney

> ... Miss May Gibbs' delightfully delicate compositions occupy a prominent place in the exhibition, which is enhanced by the presence of one of her excellent 'gum nut' illustrations.
>
> *Sydney Morning Herald*

The remainder of the year, 1922, was spent at a leisurely pace as the Kellys embarked on an increasing social life with visits to the theatre and, May's particular passion, to concerts—though not all was pleasing, as May recorded in a notebook.

> Long session Delius, Ravel, Debussy and Richard Strauss' *Don Juan.* All the lot almost could be interchanged, mixed up and come out unnoticed—the worst and most aggravating being Delius and Ravel.

With a husband's arm on which to lean, May became less socially shy and, certainly for a time, more gregarious with her peers. In August 1922, after J. O. had prepared himself with dancing lessons, the couple stepped out to the inaugural Artists' Ball. The following year the participants must have become a little too exuberant for J. O., who described it as 'a disgusting affair', resulting in their decision never to attend again. In truth it did become the bohemian gathering of the year.

May was also concentrating on the completion of a new story—*The Story of Nuttybub and Nittersing*. However, Christmas shoppers who had become confident May Gibbs would solve their shopping problem for the children each year were disappointed. There were many new merchandising items such as calendars, cards, badges and other ephemera depicting the gumnuts, but no new book.

12

A NEW PUBLISHER

Once, long ago, before the Bush creatures learned how foolish it was to wear clothes, there lived two dear little Gumnut Babies ...

Chucklebud and Wunkydoo

Upset at having to hard bargain with Angus and Robertson, May had decided to publish elsewhere and it eventuated that she had been negotiating publication of her next book, *Nuttybub and Nittersing*, with the Melbourne printers and publishers Osboldstone, who were then handling the production of enormous quantities of her calendars and cards. They were not, however, over enthusiastic about the terms she was asking.

> We have carefully read your letter in which you have clearly set out the conditions on which you have had your previous issues published. At the moment we cannot see our way to pay 15% on the published price for copies sold. As you are doubtless aware the price we would get, after allowing for intermediate profits, would be roughly about half the published price, which would be equivalent to paying you 30% on the price we get. Much as we would like to do this work for you, at present we cannot see our way to get around on these figures in justice to ourselves and you. We think 10% would be a reasonable royalty.

May, in turn, was not persuaded and Mr Benson, Osboldstone's manager, finally agreed to the author's 15 per cent royalty request. He had in addition to guarantee her a top-quality job, reproducing her art before she would sign the contract.

May had always been a perfectionist with regard to her work. Her accuracy and care, first instanced in the detailed research and execution of the illustrations for Harrap, were again evident in her drawings of the Australian bush. Flowers, leaves, insects—all were precisely observed and recorded. Once May had established her name and there was a demand for her work, she maintained, or tried to maintain, the strictest supervision over production whether it was a piece of pottery, a postcard or a book in question.

Much of her early business correspondence reveals this concern and her eye for detail as in the following request on behalf of *Little Ragged Blossom.*

> Couldn't we have a better paper for the cover—brown but nicer than the Gum-nut covers? and I'd like a much browner ink if possible.

Satisfied with assurances about paper and printing May signed the contract with Osboldstone which also gave them the right to handle her next book as soon as it was available for publication. Once confident she had won the question of royalties and quality, May concentrated on completing the two books.

But there was yet one small battle to win. Prior to publication the Osboldstone book editor felt obliged to question May's liberties with the English language.

> On page 47 of your manuscript, you have a paragraph reading 'a big sturdy little nut'. Am suggesting that you make this read 'a sturdy little nut' leaving out the 'big' as the 'big' and 'little' hardly go together.
>
> On pages 21 and 22 you spell Iguana as 'Go anna'. I understand of course that is intentional.
>
> On page 29 you have 'ater'—would suggest you make it 'arter', presumably meaning after ...

May ignored the editor and wrote to Mr Benson direct demanding that her book be left exactly as she had written it. Needless to say, it remained untouched and *Nuttybub and Nittersing* was published in 1923 priced at 6s 6d.

May's notebooks include a charming 'Note for *Nuttybub and Nittersing*' which, sadly, was never used.

> Dear Mothers and Aunties and others who may be burdened with the reading aloud of this little story.
>
> May I apologise for the ugly language of the Bad Banksia men but as they represent all that is undesirable it seemed to me unavoidable.
>
> May I suggest that you make the talk of the Frogs as Froglike as possible and the voice of Mr Lizard very eccentric, elderly and, kind. The speech of the Big White Bird is meant to be, tho' humorous, decidedly Impressive. It embodies my hatred of how things are imprisoned, especially birds whose chief characteristic is that of flight.

May's concern for bush creatures and her campaign on their behalf were in advance of many in her time. She preached kindness to plants and animals in almost all she drew and wrote. Her concern was recognised and, in 1919, May Gibbs was made a life member of the Royal Society for the Prevention of Cruelty to Animals.

Nuttybub and Nittersing are two more gumnuts who live in the Australian bush.

> Yes, they are very hard to see, but they are building their houses, making their bread, and minding their children in the daytime and climbing into their beds and going to sleep at night ... Just like Humans.

Nuttybub introduces himself to a wasp, and the young reader learns about the eating habits of this insect. May spared her youthful audience none of the grim realities of life which were always part of the danger and excitement of her stories.

> 'Who are you?' questioned the wasp.
> 'I'm a Gumnut,' answered Nuttybub.
> 'It's well for you because I was just going to sting you and then you'd have slept till my babies were big enough to eat you up.'

In this story, for the first time, children actually learn the height of a gumnut.

> He made his way to the brook. Of course, a brook seemed like a river to Nuttybub. You must remember he was only two inches high.

For the first time also there is biological data on the dreaded Banksia Men.

> From far and near they come, all sorts and kinds of Wild Bad Banksia Men. Long thin red ones; great Knobbly, brown ones; fat, round, green and grey ones, short thick black ones; yellow ones, and some almost white.

Nuttybub and Nittersing, released during August 1923, was to earn some of the finest reviews May had yet received.

> The books of May Gibbs are on the way to becoming classics of Australian childhood. Her skill in sketching gumnut babies, brownies and all the other fairy stories which she weaves about the wee folk (or is it that the pictures grow up about the stories) are equally clear and delightful. Nuttybub and Nittersing are worthy successors to our old friends Snugglepot and Cuddlepie. Perhaps,

indeed they were all along in the kingdom which we previously explored, but our too human eyes overlooked them—naturally enough.

Daily Telegraph, Sydney

New Gumnut Book ... Of Miss May Gibbs, this paper has long thought that among Australian writers for children, she is liveliest, daintiest and best and there are few writers in the world with minds so sweetly attuned to that of a child. It is good news for those who sleep in little cots that Miss Gibbs has published another book filled with Gumnut people who triumph over nasty Banksia men and Good Natured Mr Lizard still helping to defeat the enemy.

Sunday Times, London

May Gibbs is really more important to Australian children than *Alice in Wonderland*. Every Christmas she tells, and illustrates, a fairy story of the great Gumnut family. The telling is as charming as the pictures, for fortunately, this artist will never grow up. There is something seriously wrong with any child who does not appreciate the humour of the telling or the delight of the pictures in each succeeding instalment of this perennial saga of the eucalyptus. Every full page is packed with the delicate and humorous detail that children love to pore over and it would be a cross-grained old parent who would not smile at the 'Gumflower Ball'. The latest instalment is called *Nuttybub and Nittersing*.

Sun, Sydney

Kidnapped by the bad Banksia men! The inventiveness of the author is equal to a most amusing flow of encounters, with birds and beasts, and the two babies manage to have a rattling good time before the book is ended. There is real comic inspiration in some of the illustrations, and the story is written with a rare understanding of the youthful mind.

Telegraph, Brisbane

Miss May Gibbs who, in her own way, has contributed much towards Australian folklore, has issued yet another compilation of fairy stories. May Gibbs has the true knack of adapting Australian flora and fauna to fairy ruse.

Punch

May Gibbs possesses the rare gift of entertaining by the imagination and originality so gracefully blended in her works. Tiny ones who cannot read will love to gaze upon the illustrations which crowd the book. These stories are cunningly and painlessly instructive, as

> are all the illustrations of life in Gumnut Land. Even the grown up folk will find delight in the irresistible daintiness of such pictures as the Gumnut concert, and its beautiful prima donna, the dance of the Brolgas and the shopping scene. Miss May Gibbs as artist and writer, is a better advertisement for Australia than half a dozen propagandists.
>
> *Daily Mail*, Perth

Published in 1924, a year after *Nuttybub*, and fully titled *Two Little Gumnuts — Chucklebud and Wunkydoo Their Strange Adventures, Chucklebud and Wunkydoo*, as the book became known, was to be the last of the gumnut adventure stories. It was much shorter than the earlier books. For many critics *Chucklebud and Wunkydoo* did not come up to the standard of the previous stories. Though like its predecessors it contained the eternal fight of good against evil, with the gumnuts as inventive as ever in outwitting the Banksia Men, some of the more unusual names caused confusion among some readers.

It was difficult to explain the ultimate failure of the two books. Sales of *Nuttybub and Nittersing* had taken off at first, as did sales for *Chucklebud and Wunkydoo*, then demand for the books ceased, and so too did the May Gibbs-Osboldstone venture. The publishers were at a loss to explain the failure, although May appeared to accept the disappointment philosophically.

> Please let me have the original drawings. I am, of course, very sorry our joint venture has turned out so unsatisfactorily, especially as the books were turned out so beautifully and carefully. I can only think it is a matter of price.

Despite their failure in bookstores, Nuttybub and Nittersing were not entirely lost to children in New South Wales. In 1927 the Education Department of that state ran an extract which covered the gumnuts' first adventure in their issue of 1 April. Two years later, in 1929, *Nuttybub and Nittersing* and *Chucklebud and Wunkydoo* were also released in small editions by Angus and Robertson with their brother books. A revamped *Chucklebud and Wunkydoo — Those Inquisitive Gumnut Babies*, was printed by Angus and Robertson in 1932 and, although it was during the depression years, the pantomime theatricals of the pair proved more popular with the later generation.

In addition to supervising the production of the two books, May spent a great deal of the year pursuing her interest in portrait painting. The portraits were watercolours and it is not known how many of them still exist. Known subjects were the family—Cecilia, Herbert, J. O., Rene and herself. Others were of conductor-pianist Cherniavsky; violinist Jascha Heifetz; Levitsky, an antique and art collector; James Chuey, described by J. O. as 'a Chinese baron' of the period; and Moiseiwitsch, the pianist. A portrait of a neighbour, Mr Stavenhagen, is in the possession of the Art Gallery of New South Wales, presented to them by his daughter. Miss Stavenhagen related her memories of May Gibbs.

> Sitting on the balcony she sketched away for hours ... I was considered a well-behaved child so I was allowed to stand and watch her work. I was perfectly happy there. She drew quickly and, if some little thing did not please her, she did it over and over and got up and walked around the room. Then I'd get out very quickly without saying BOO.

May's portrait period culminated with a painting of Dr Throsby, a North Sydney physician. She was particularly pleased with the result and, encouraged by her husband, submitted it to the Society of Artists' show. To her disappointment, it was rejected, and she refused to submit any more, deeply hurt by the criticism of her portrait work.

In fact, it appears that it was difficult for May to take criticism or direction at any time. On this occasion she excused her retreat by laying the blame on the antagonism and competition which, she felt, prevailed on that section of the art world.

She now had eight children's books published and the Snugglepot and Cuddlepie adventures were well on the way to becoming classics of Australian children's literature. She thus returned to the world of her bush babies where she ruled supreme.

13
CARTOONIST AND COLUMNIST

Gumnut Editors generally write backwards, because they say it takes longer to read and that way the people think they are getting more news.

Tales of Snugglepot and Cuddlepie

The creator of Bib and Bub faces the challenge of a blank page, 1923.

Despite the fact that J. O. recorded in his diary that it was a bad year, 1924 was one of the most significant years in his wife's career, as May Gibbs was to join the ranks of Australia's cartoonists. She would later be regarded as one of the most talented and prolific members of this gifted group.

The comic strip was becoming an established favourite with Australian children and the cartoon was one of May's favourite forms of expression, as the hundreds of cartoon cards she had been producing for correspondence with friends and relatives over the years testify.

The pioneer of the Australian comic strip was Stan Cross, an American-born Australian, who also grew up in Perth. Some eleven years May Gibbs' junior, Stan was undoubtedly as aware of Gibbs' work as she was of his.

Working in Sydney in 1919, Stan Cross created Australia's first comic strip cartoon, 'You and Me', which was later to become 'The Potts' and was taken over by Jim Russell. 'You and Me' was published in *Smith's Weekly*, whose managing director was Robert Clyde Packer. Two years later, Jim Bancks supplied 'Us Fellers', later to become 'Ginger Meggs', to the Sydney newspaper, the Sydney *Sun*. Syd Nicholls followed with a strip for the *Sunday News*, 'Fat and His Friends', which appeared in 1923 and eventually developed into the children's favourite, 'Fatty Finn'.

May Gibbs had learnt the importance of wisely placing your product and, after an analysis of the market, decided the best outlet for her cartoons was the *Sunday News*.

The editor of this newspaper was Errol Knox (later to be knighted). He, like the majority of Australians, was familiar with May Gibbs, the author, but May Gibbs, the cartoonist, was an unknown quantity. When May was ushered into his office, Knox saw a middle-aged woman, well dressed in the fashion of the day with her hair bobbed under a tight fitting hat. She was short in stature, though tall in presence and had a keen knowledge of the many subjects they discussed. He was delighted to find that she was an entertaining conversationalist, with a background in journalistic illustration covering some twenty years.

When Knox perused the contents of the folder she presented, May knew 'The Gumnuts' had him intrigued. She watched the editor's face soften as he read the comic strips and finally he made the one comment, 'Too simple'. Then he quickly sent for his senior artist, Syd Nicholls.

Syd, a young Tasmanian, was to spend his life completely dedicated to the promotion of the Australian cartoonist. He vividly remembered the interview with Mrs Kelly, when speaking of her half a century later.

> Mrs Kelly seemed to me a bit of an old bird to be entering the comic strip game in her mid-forties. Anyway I looked at her work. The gumnuts were quite unique, there was nothing like them in the world. They were not fairies, they were not caricatures, but reflected everyone we know.
>
> From an artistic standpoint alone, her work had all the essentials of fine workmanship, perspective, anatomy, structure and composition, with the simplicity of a talented cartoonist. Why not? She was a graduate of the Blackburn School of Arts in London, when I was a kid.
>
> I wondered if she could keep up the pace for newspaper deadlines, but that was Knox's problem. When I looked up, her twinkling brown eyes returned my gaze with a puckish grin of confidence that later confirmed my opinion—she could read your mind. My reply to Knox's unasked question was, 'When does Mrs Kelly start?'. My editor replied, 'Why not now!'

For the sum of five pounds per strip, May Gibbs was to supply a half page cartoon strip each week, with at least four strips in advance of the publication date. The contract was to be renewed after twelve months and contained a mutual notice of cancellation clause. Knox allowed May to retain syndication rights and the right to publish the cartoons in book form.

'Bib and Bub', first published in August 1925, adopted the European comic-strip format, the text being placed beneath each panel. May's hand-lettered captions were a style of scribbly-gum printing. After a few weeks, the straight story lines were replaced with May's verses which she appears to have preferred to prose and found easier to write. Her notebooks are crammed with verses which seem to have been effortlessly dashed off with very little correction and, except for two instances, no hesitation over rhyme. In contrast, her notebook experiments in prose are far less sure and bear the emendation which is not unexpected in draft material.

May's rhymes and experimental word sounds and her illustrations revealing an eye for the ridiculous combined to present small lessons in life for her young audience. When it was pointed out her strips were being used for reading lessons and pupils had difficulty reading the less formal scribbly-gum letters, a little less reluctantly than was her usual response to requests for change, May allowed the publishers to typeset the verse.

The strip proved a financial success as well as a popular one and provided a source of revenue that was to surpass the income from the gumnut books. The *Adelaide Mail* took it in its first month of publication for £4 4s. By November 'Bib and Bub' was appearing across the Tasman in the *New Zealand Herald,* Auckland, returning the cartoonist £4, and a Melbourne paper, the *Star,* purchased it for £3 3s.

The following year, Queenslanders read it in the *Northern Queensland Register,* Townsville, and the return was £3. The *Daily Mail,* in Brisbane, purchased it for a negotiated price of £2 12s 6d.

The weekly appearance of the 'Bib and Bub' cartoons must take some credit for supporting the popularity of the story books through the ensuing years.

May Gibbs' ability to entertain her new public over a two-year period was rewarded with a contract commissioning a full page cartoon of the gumnuts, with the increased fee of £10 per strip.

In 1926, the *Daily News* in her home town, Perth, secured the Western Australian rights and, although they had been tardy in doing so—they followed the rest of Australia—they waxed eloquent when announcing the strip's appearance:

> Charming drawings and delightful humour have made this series the most popular feature appearing in any Australian paper. May Gibbs has struck a distinctive note, all Australian, and quite free of the vulgarity which marks so many of the allegedly comic strips which are supposed to amuse the younger generation.

The success of the 'Bib and Bub' cartoon convinced the editor of the *Sunday News* that Mrs Kelly had a way with entertaining children and, when she presented him with a short story, the first in a proposed series, for the children's section of the newspaper, he agreed to print it. Errol Knox had come to admire the Gibbs style and viewed the proposal as eminently suitable for expanding the children's supplement of the *Sunday News.*

'Gumnut Gossip—Extracts from the *Daily Bark*' was 'translated by May Gibbs', and appeared in August 1925. It had a newspaper style about it and recorded short reports and stories, always with a humorous twist or moral for its readers, of the doings and gossip of Gumnut Town. Now, May Gibbs was back to painting pictures with words rather than drawings, though the author did support her story with a small illustration.

The *Daily Bark,* a Gumnut Town newspaper, first appeared in *Tales of Snugglepot and Cuddlepie,* with comments explaining the idiosyncrasies of gumnut editors, quoted above: '... people think they are getting more news'.

In truth many children were 'getting more' and the column became a boon to many families whose basic literature was the newspaper. Astute gumnut fans could detect that some of the stories were adaptations from ideas already published in the 'Bib and Bub' cartoon series but most of the ideas were original and, in turn, some 'Gumnut Gossip' stories were a source of inspiration for 'Bib and Bub' cartoons.

Errol Knox, negotiating the contract, agreed to a fee of thirty shillings per column. Like the cartoon strip, 'Gumnut Gossip' was syndicated to papers throughout Australia and became part of Australia's weekly reading.

From 1925 to 1930 the *Sunday News* printed 205 'Gumnut Gossip' stories, until the merger of the *News* and the *Guardian*, when the column was transferred to the *Woman's Budget*, a popular woman's magazine of its day.

During the latter part of 1930 to 1932, May Gibbs the columnist produced particularly good work. Of the 141 stories printed in that period, titles like 'The Little Old Desk', 'Staghorns and Elks', 'The Friend from India', 'Captain Platypus' and 'Mud Worms' convey the variety of subjects touched on by the author. Some stories were completed in one issue and others were serialised. All of them were entertaining and thinking teachers of the day used them to supplement reading material. Books and stories which communicated about life in Australia to young Australians were rare.

Each story graphically portrayed the characteristics of its subjects in a few short words and used liberal slangish exclamations, such as 'Spit and splinter!', 'My bully ant!', 'Bless my bones!'.

Reminiscing one day with Win Preston about the days on The Harvey property, May recalled the country characters she had experimented with and, rifling through a huge cedar box, which housed a host of ideas, came across sketches of what she called her 'pig era'.

The various pigs of May's imagination vied for stardom in what was to be another cartoon strip and the eventual leading lady came forward as the roughest and ugliest of creatures. A childhood memory of a name from English folklore, 'Tiggy', provided the first name, and the magic word 'Touchwood' became the pig's surname. The cartoon strip was again directed to the very young reader.

Interviewers were always curious as to which came first with May Gibbs, the pictures or the verse, and she was obliged to confess that, although she dearly loved to be thought of as an author, the pictures came first.

The new idea was presented to Errol Knox, who was more than happy at the prospect of a new May Gibbs cartoon for the *Sunday News.* Her relationship with the paper was extremely good. Her work, professionally executed, was always delivered on schedule, the content was always entertaining and Syd Nicholls was aware of the constancy of her quality and her succinct observations. With her usual concern for perfection there were, of course, a few tussles with the etcher, stereotyper and printer reproducing her work, but the *News*' staff had given in to her wishes. They had learned from experience that 'the old bird invariably got what she wanted'.

The 'Tiggy Touchwood' cartoon, however, was something of a shock to Errol Knox. He had naturally expected to see beautifully shaped gumnuts and wildflowers in a new setting but the new character was a complete departure from previous work. Tiggy Touchwood was a pipe-smoking pig with a witch's talent for magic. Her companions were two little koalas, whom Tiggy found in the introductory strip.

Somewhat taken aback by the new presentation, Knox wondered if she had grown tired of the gumnuts and hastened to assure her that the management was extremely happy with the 'Bib and Bub' adventures and that readers were calling for more. When May explained that 'Tiggy Touchwood' was not intended to replace her other series but was another project, Knox could not see the *Sunday News* comic section handling two strips for young readers and had to refuse May's new cartoon.

It was a great disappointment to the Kellys and, after much debate, they decided to try the rival paper, the *Sunday Sun.*

The editor of the *Sunday Sun* was only too pleased to accept a May Gibbs product but Errol Knox was not happy about one of his contributors placing a cartoon with a rival newspaper. He aired his misgivings to Syd Nicholls who, now a staunch champion of 'the little English lady', assured his editor that, if anyone could serve two newspapers with quite different cartoons, it was Mrs Kelly. He also reminded Knox that, despite the popularity of the gumnuts, the newspaper management had not rewarded the artist with a penny more in her new contract and it was unfair to restrict her to one publication.

> 'Mrs Kelly deserves every chance she can get. There isn't anyone else trying to provide material for the really tiny ones.'

Knox compromised with the stipulation that Mrs Kelly had to use a nom de plume. May Gibbs worked for the *News* and he did not want her name to be featured in the *Sunday Sun.*

Despite her efforts to hide her sex behind a pseudonym early in her career, May was not really happy about the use of a nom de plume. Now the name May Gibbs was established, she resented the need to hide behind another identity. However, on 5 September 1925, the *Sunday Sun* featured a new cartoon by an unknown artist, Stan Cottman, but it did not take long for the shrewd cartoon buff to recognise the artist. The distinctive wildflowers and the idiosyncratic humour may have given a clue—within a few weeks, many readers realised 'Tiggy Touchwood' was the world of the creator of the gumnuts. May Gibbs became the only artist to have a weekly cartoon strip in rival newspapers.

By May 1926, 'Tiggy Touchwood' was to appear in the Melbourne *Sunday News Pictorial* and Victorian readers joined her many admirers, and in fact 'Tiggy Touchwood' was more popular there than 'Bib and Bub'.

Tiggy was a unique character who, in addition to bringing her adventures to readers in rhythm and rhyme, introduced a touch of magic. Although cartoon readers were aware of the gumnuts' beginnings, having gumnut story books to refer to, Tiggy's origins were not revealed until the release of a May Gibbs' story titled *Mr and Mrs Bear and Friends* in 1943. For eighteen years no one knew Tiggy Touchwood was really a princess.

The success of the May Gibbs' newspaper cartoons led to a renewal of interest from Angus and Robertson, who advanced £100 against future royalty earnings and published the first May Gibbs cartoon book, titled *Bib and Bub Their Adventures, Part 1*, in 1925. The cartoon book for the very young was an instant success, selling 4893 copies at 4s 6d each. This time, the publisher and May had agreed on a 12½ per cent royalty. *Wee Gumnut Babies — Bib and Bub, Part 2* followed in the same year as did a hard-bound copy combining both books. Then came *Further Adventures of Bib and Bub* (1927), *More Funny Stories about Old Friends Bib and Bub* (1928), and *Bib and Bub in Gumnut Town* (1929).

While enthusiasm for the cartoons grew, a slump in sales of all the gumnut books was experienced during this period, particularly of the two which had been published by Osboldstone, *Nuttybub and Nittersing* and *Chucklebud and Wunkydoo.*

Angus and Robertson made another approach to May, offering to take over her Osboldstone publications, and eventually they bought up some 9000 books at a sadly reduced rate. It was a tremendous blow to the author's pride but, for business reasons, the Kellys agreed to the transfer.

Now all the gumnut books were in the same stable together with the cartoon books. The quality of the cartoon books distressed May greatly but she was in no position to demand more of their reproduction, though as the following portion of a letter to George Robertson shows, that did not deter her from trying.

> Dear Mr Robertson,
>
> ...
>
> 4 Do not let the Babies be suffering from measles as in the cover design of old B. and B.!! as this is very distressing to their mother.
> 5 Let all the inks be strong and dark in the inside pages; discard any colour that inclines to paleness.
> 6 Give me nice colours in the dust jacket, it will pay.
> I hope that's all.
>
> Very sincerely
> May Gibbs (The Truant)

There was only one professional disappointment during this period. May suggested to Angus and Robertson in 1928 that they produce a book of the 'Gumnut Gossip' stories but the idea was rejected.

The end of the twenties was a prosperous period, and a prolific one. A weekly cartoon strip for 'Bib and Bub', a weekly cartoon strip for 'Tiggy Touchwood', and a weekly column, 'Gumnut Gossip', three books of cartoons, *Further Adventures of Bib and Bub, More Funny Stories about Bib and Bub* and *Bib and Bub in Gumnut Town,* plus contributions to the New South Wales and Queensland State School Education Department magazines kept the creator at her drawing board.

In his book on Australian cartoons, *Panel by Panel* (1979), John Ryan surveyed May's achievement.

> [Bib and Bub] was the most successful of any strip (local or imported) aimed at very juvenile readers ... Her clean, crisp line drawings and soft water colours were accurate and instructive and she never lost sight of the fact that she was drawing for the very young.

May, the successful cartoonist and columnist.

14
MRS KELLY

I know his good points and disappoints
Notebook jotting

Reminiscing, friends and relatives a generation or more behind May and J. O. recall their youthfully irreverent impressions of them as 'a funny old couple', and an oddly assorted pair who were never alone together.

In truth, once J. O. had accepted the unusual home arrangements of sharing the Runnymede flat with Rene and Rachel, there was seldom to be a time when the Kellys were alone. Even on holiday trips, some friend or relative was always invited along or in residence. It was obvious that May had no desire to set up a conventional home. Perhaps the experience of her Perth home lifestyle left her with a liking for communal living and, as her friends recalled, she always liked to be surrounded by people. Although she was always reserved with strangers, she liked an audience and enjoyed being the centre of an admiring circle.

J. O. was just part of that circle and, as those who knew her recollect, he was not the most important of her relationships. Rene, Rachel and, most dear, her father had all a greater call on her affections than James Ossoli Kelly.

The ménage at Runnymede was only to last a year before moving to larger quarters in Derry, Phillip Street, Neutral Bay. Soon after came a major and unexpected disruption. Rene married fellow post-office employee, Joe Sullivan, and departed with him to the country town of Bombala. This was undoubtedly a great rift in May's life, although she was always to maintain the closest contact with Rene who continued to visit for long periods and was always to be relied on in times of trouble.

To assist with the rent the Kellys and Rachel then shared the house with an English couple, the Lukes, with whom they had become friendly but when, later, the Lukes returned to England, May decided to utilise the additional space and transferred the Little Studio from the city across the harbour to the house.

Also, with room to spare now at Derry, Cecilie and Herbert were enticed to New South Wales for a holiday which was to extend for almost a year.

They were happy months both for May and her parents, although Cecie, noted in the family for acute perception, may have begun to have misgivings about her son-in-law. J. O. had presented himself much as a man of independent means, although there is little to suggest he brought any money into the marriage. J. O. was expected to earn his keep by looking after his wife's finances.

Perhaps, like her daughter, Cecie may have had the impression that J. O. had a private income but it was now obvious that he was dependent on May and was handling May's money and her steadily growing bank balance. Cecie's concern was translated into action and she intervened with plans to invest the money safely in real estate. Knowing this would be challenged by J. O., who preferred to rent rather than taking on the responsibilities of a mortgage, she made her enquiries discreetly. When she had selected a suitable block of waterfront land—at No. 5 Wallaringa Avenue, Neutral Bay—she commenced negotiations and then, satisfied the deal could be finalised, casually informed the rest of the family about it during dinner one night. She lightened the situation with stories of one of the Kellys' Scottish terriers christening a gum tree and putting his seal of approval on the property, but both May and J. O. were aware of her conniving. Fortunately, J. O. accepted the situation without protest and a large deposit was put on the property.

May, too, might have been forgiven for having misgivings about her husband. While he looked after her accounts with punctiliousness and skill, he had failed, by the artist's determined standards, to prove a resolute negotiator. As he had shown when negotiations for *Little Obelia* were in progress, when dealing with publishers he showed a possibly genteel dislike of the bargaining May believed necessary to ensure her rights. She had had to fight her own battles with Angus and Robertson and Osboldstone, and though she was a great and generally triumphant battler in this arena, she, too, always found the role distasteful.

It would not have been surprising if J. O.'s lifestyle when they were first married led to some disappointment as well. At Runnymede J. O. had the flat to himself during the day and spent the time with his books, following the stock exchange and mineral market reports and sorting out May's accounts. This business

Cecilia and Herbert pay a visit to May at Nutcote.

routine was interspersed with visits to Aaron's Hotel in the city, to hear the latest trends in the sharemarket, and to the best outfitters where he indulged his fondness for fine clothes, after which he would escort his wife home at the end of the day. He was living the life of a gentleman while his wife, if not struggling, was pursuing with keen commercial acumen many outlets to make a living from her art and her creations.

Despite whatever fractiousness there might have been in the early days of their marriage and the unconventionality of the relationship, their partnership was to survive—they were to become 'the best of pals'. J. O. provided May with a handsome social prop, a convivial partner to offset her shyness, and a champion on her behalf in all but negotiation. He widened the circle of their friends and acquaintances and, with his support, May began to move out into society and particularly that of her artistic peers.

Once the Kellys had built their own house, however, their home once again became the important centre of their social life.

Said Bib to Bub, 'We'll build her a house.'
So they borrowed a saw from the carpenter mouse.

The axe was swung by kind Mr Roo
Mr Platypus told them what to do . . .

The talented and fashionable architect, B. J. Waterhouse, transferred May's wishes for compactness, convenience and charm into a Spanish-type villa. Perched on a steep slope on the eastern side of Neutral Bay, the yellow cottage with blue shutters looked past a huge gum tree at the afternoon sun. The grass at the end of the sloping grounds led to the harbour waters and provided an ideal area for a swimming pool. Cecilia had chosen well!

The house boasted a long living room, leading out on to an arched balcony. Right of the balcony was a dining room with views from every window, and on the left, sunlit by bay windows looking across the harbour, was the studio where May Gibbs was to spend the rest of her working life. Two bedrooms, a dressing room, kitchen, and all conveniences completed upstairs, while downstairs was a smaller living area. At street level was a double garage with a tiny flatette beneath.

The architect asked the author to call the house Nutcote and she obliged him. With their two Scotty dogs, Jamie and Peter, the Kellys took up residence in February 1925.

At Nutcote they were to establish a lifestyle very reminiscent of that of The Dune in Perth. It was a gathering place particularly for old friends and family. Despite his initial misgivings, J. O. enjoyed the house immensely and delighted in playing host. While the subjects for conversation were universal, politics invariably led F. E. de Groot, a constant visitor, into a debate on bolshevism and J. O. found that he and the Irish royalist shared similar ideas. Long before de Groot had 'carved' a name for himself by unofficially opening the Sydney Harbour Bridge, he had become a regular visitor to Nutcote and, in the thirties, eventually influenced J. O. to join the New Guard.

Politics had never interested May and the animated discussions, leading, as they so often did, to heated clashes between J. O. and Rene—the right wing and the left—were always distressing to her. Her own philosophy is perhaps best expressed in a notebook jotting from 1934.

> This terrible energy of mind that makes men build miracles in machinery to massacre men in millions. And other men miracles in medicine to mend them again. You keep your eyes on the world,

> I keep mine on my own Garden. Is it going to be any good, any better when everybody learns to look at the world instead of into their own little cabbage patch.

Her preference for her own cabbage patch notwithstanding, May held her own in other areas of conversation as is recorded in an article in the *Australian Home Journal* in March 1926.

> But she will not talk about her work. Art, music, books, clothes, housekeeping, any of these, yes. An exquisite watercolour portrait hung in a modest corner, for instance, will draw an admiring remark or question, but Mrs Kelly deftly changes the subject. Only looking at her now and again one feels her attention wander, that behind the talk in which she takes such a brilliant part, she is listening to a woodland harmony, an elusive, distracting fairy music, such as ordinary mortals wot not of, but to which her truly Australian fairies dance to the delight of Australia's children.

May only allowed herself sparing time with those who came to stay or called in and, after entertaining them for the period she had allocated, would leave her guests and retreat to her studio. Then she went to work, sometimes capturing the personalities of the friends she had just left, a story she had just heard or a subject she had just discussed, weaving them into the adventures of her gumnuts.

Rene's wedding present to May and J. O. had been an adorable puppy, Shamus, who was not unlike Wog of May Gibbs' first story book. He was a Scottish terrier May had admired at a show and she became devoted to him and immortalised him in print. 'Shamus' was to be followed by a steady flow of Scottish terriers who shared the rest of the Kellys' life.

May was always reluctant to part with all the puppies from a litter and so the family of Scotties gradually increased. The pets placed a restriction on their holidaying together so that the Kellys were gradually forced to take separate vacations. While J. O.'s favourite jaunt was to Queanbeyan, trout fishing, May would stay with Rene wherever she and Joe were stationed or take off to her beloved Blue Mountains.

Behind Sydney is the blue eucalyptus-laden range which provides a bushy escape from city life. When chasing inspiration, May often boarded the train and headed for these mountains, recording them in her work and in her notebook jottings.

> Wonder of the delicate tissue paper-like bark of the paper bark tree, white grey, flesh colour and cream tints in their straight layers one above the other. During a short stop I could see a still pool, reflecting a group of paperbarks. The dark foliage, deep green behind white Japanese type stems was most lovely.

May did give some thought to having a home there and purchased a couple of blocks of land at Blackheath. The area had become very fashionable among artists from Sydney, particularly with the faster train services, but J. O. found it all 'jolly but very cold'.

On one of May's trips to Wentworth Falls, she travelled in Win Preston's new car and was captivated by the vehicle. By the time they arrived back in Neutral Bay, May was animated by the prospect of having her own transport. Thus J. O. was instructed to find a suitable automobile and, although he tried to point out that the motor car had been responsible for the deaths of three of their Scotty dogs and they had both agreed never to own one, May cut his protests short with the declaration that she wanted one as quickly as possible. J. O., recognising the finality in the voice, did as he was commanded and, with an eye for a bargain settled on a second-hand Dodge Tourer for £195.

May could not wait to get her hands on the wheel or her feet on the pedals, quite an accomplishment in itself considering the structure of the cars of the day and her stature. After a couple of days' manoeuvring the 'Dodgem', she considered she had had sufficient tuition to obtain her licence.

The prowess of both the Kellys as drivers was suspect. Both Cecilia and Herbert were enticed into the 'Dodgem' during one of their lengthy visits to Nutcote and, after a rather exhausting trip to Palm Beach and back, Mrs Gibbs, with a directness often displayed by her daughter, graciously refused any more adventures in the 'Dodgem'. J. O. described the parents' drive as 'their first and last'.

The Kellys were not deterred. She was the pilot, J. O. the navigator and, if there were no other passengers, the Scotty dogs occupied the back seat. If guests were aboard, the Scotty family pushed their noses against the inside of the wicker baskets arranged on the running boards either side of the car.

The beautiful environs of Sydney were still a bushland covered with wildflowers and inhabited by bush creatures, and Pennant Hills, Dural, Hornsby and Galston Gorge were all Kelly haunts.

Further afield, their favourite locations were Bowral, the mountains and Laurieton.

There is no question that the 'Dodgem' was one of the great joys of May's life. She delighted in being able to take off for a trip into the country and, at a leisurely pace, being able to observe the bushland. Frequent stops were made to boil the billy, let the dogs go for a run, or simply study a scene or incident which captured the driver's fancy.

Like her father, May always carried a notebook. Miniature sketches and notes of a scene or area were made frequently and, in weeks following the trip, the material appeared in one of her assignments.

As veterans of the New South Wales roads, the Kellys were most impressed when May's brother, Ivan, and Calanchini drove across from Perth in 1927. They stayed at Nutcote but, when invited for drives around Sydney, were quick to manoeuvre the Kellys into their car for the excursions. It was only when they returned to Perth May realised they had always travelled in the Western Australian car and observed, 'I didn't get a chance to take them for a ride in the Dodgem.'

May with the famous 'Dodgem' at Galston Gorge, late 1920s.

15
LEAN YEARS

We get very near the breadline ... must seriously think of some sort of labour.

J. O. Kelly, letter

The depression of the thirties was to affect all Australians but perhaps none more so than those working in the arts. Books, paintings, music—all could be regarded as luxuries, and their creators must have felt their existence a perilous one. In common with her peers, May experienced cutbacks in income, and it was a financial blow from which the inhabitants of Nutcote never quite recovered.

May's agents, The Special Press, were responsible for the cartoonist's contracts from the date of the release of 'Bib and Bub' in August 1924. Despite the fact that pleasantries were constantly exchanged between the city office and Nutcote, the Kellys rather resented the 25 per cent agent's commission and often discussed the advisability of keeping on with the service.

In February 1930, the *Guardian* took over the *Sunday News* and, with it, May Gibbs' contract for a full-page 'Bib and Bub'. But 20 April of the same year, the strip was reduced to a half-page format, which distressed the author greatly, and her fee was reduced to half the previous rate, which upset her business manager even more. Unfortunately, no attempt had been made by her agents to obtain a new contract with the *Guardian* and theirs was the responsibility for this reduction.

The slight of having her work reduced sparked a discontent May had not felt for some years, indeed, not since the Angus and Robertson royalty confrontation. Whether or not she had forgotten the drastic results of that battle, prudence was not evident in her consequent action.

At the outset her relationship with the rival newspaper, *Sunday Sun*, was an amicable one. They were happy with 'Tiggy Touchwood' and the managing director, H. Campbell-Jones, was fulsome in praise.

> We think that Miss Gibbs goes from strength to strength and the writer personally enjoys nothing more than his Sunday absorption of her whimsical and delightful ideas.
>
> And again, in response to a Christmas strip:
>
> One of the marvels of the World is the manner in which you maintain the splendid standard of your most effective children's comic. It did not seem possible to achieve any more fascinating entertainment than you have provided weekly throughout the year, but your Christmas strip would, I am sure, bear comparison with the very best that any artist turned out in any part of the world.

Unfortunately, this atmosphere of goodwill was undermined. Early in 1930, at much the same time as the *Guardian* troubles, the Kellys discovered that the *Sunday Sun* had been syndicating 'Tiggy Touchwood' in New Zealand without reference to the author.

Following a visit to their offices, where she was informed Mr Campbell-Jones was not in (which she did not believe), she impulsively resigned from the paper, thereby turning the managing director from an admirer to a hurt employer.

> Your New Year's gift—notice of discontinuance—is the worst that has come my way, but being an Englishman, I can fully understand your 'pull' to the homeland. I am fairly confident that you can create a very pleasant place for yourself in London Journalism and it will be a pleasure to help you in any way I can.

Without the constant comings and goings of relatives and friends from overseas, the Kellys' return to England was a project forever discussed. It was, however, without any real substance and the proposed move to England was a bluff.

However, threat to take legal action was real enough and her solicitor at the law firm Roxburgh & Company was not unused to sorting out the infringements of May's copyright. The argument with Campbell-Jones was resolved. May withdrew her resignation though the *Sunday Sun* had to settle for the New Zealand misdemeanour.

The Special Press were dismissed as May Gibbs' journalistic agents, finalising a business arrangement that had really been a most profitable one for her. For the following year, established contracts were to continue, and although the Kellys constantly appreciated the additional 25 per cent in the fees, J. O.'s workload was increased and they were now forced to hire him an assistant.

Regarding the release of her agent, May wrote to Campbell-Jones:

> I hasten to reply because I do not wish [you] to read into my formal letter of notice of discontinuance with The Special Press any suggestion that I suspect either dishonesty or inefficiency.
>
> Apparently there are misunderstandings between us in a great many matters, and I find it very hard to do my work with such an atmosphere surrounding me.
>
> I think it better that I should be in direct contact with the Editor of the Paper I work with.

Leaving the new assistant in charge, May and J. O. took a prolonged holiday in the bush. Their trip was to take them through Laurieton and Port Macquarie to Dungog, camping all the way. By design, they avoided hotels and any contact with civilisation, preferring to camp in the peace of the bush.

The May Gibbs assignments continued to make their deadlines to the newspapers and school magazines while the Kellys enjoyed their holiday, oblivious of the gloom creeping into the newspapers as the world economy faltered.

On return to Nutcote the Kellys were to feel the first impact of the depression. May proceeded to her studio to unload the notes and sketches she had been collecting throughout the holiday, a feast of ideas for her comic strips, while J. O. settled down to one of his favourite tasks, opening the mail and meticulously arranging the contents into various categories.

The relaxing occupation was brought to a nervous halt when he opened a letter from the *Woman's Budget*, which contained the information that they wished to reduce the 'Gumnut Gossip' fee to £1 1s. Another letter, in a semicircularised form, announced the forthcoming takeover of the *Guardian*, which raised the spectre of a further reduction in earnings. The *Adelaide Mail*, in a much more civilised vein, requested a reduced rate. J. O. was understandably hesitant about relaying this ominous news to his wife.

> I fully appreciate the fact that we have all to suffer the results of the depression, [she replied to the *Adelaide Mail*] and I sincerely hope that the clouds will soon clear away. I am getting hit left and right.

The previous year had been a most successful one financially, the return of £2068 in newspaper fees alone being the highest

May had yet received, and the Kellys could perhaps have been forgiven for anticipating that this success would continue.

When Associated Newspapers Limited took over the *Guardian* and merged it with the *Sunday Sun* in 1931, two of May Gibbs' strips, 'Bib and Bub' and 'Tiggy Touchwood', appeared in the same newspaper. In the *Guardian*, 'Bib and Bub' had enjoyed the front page in the comic section but in the *Sunday Sun*, this front page was solely occupied by 'Ginger Meggs' and nothing would make the editor, Eric Baume, accede to the demands of the forthright lady, who was claiming the front page for her gumnuts, not the least concerned with the legal complications of displacing 'Ginger Meggs'.

In the final confrontation, Eric Baume was to declare that the fur-wrapped figure which ranted and raved in his office was not unlike one of her own bush creatures. May noted tersely:

> Brainwave from *Sun* (Baume & Wannecky, etc)
> Turn bears into Bib and Bub and make that
> one feature. Tig and Bib and Bub. NO!
> 2nd brainwave from *Sun*.
> Put B & B in *Budget*. NO!

As a result of the confrontation, not only did 'Bib and Bub' lose the front page position but a reduction in fee was announced, resulting in May's decision to withdraw the cartoon, which she did late in 1931. In her annoyance, she also decided to retire completely from the Sydney press and forwarded a resignation on behalf of 'Tiggy Touchwood' to the managing director of Associated Newspapers Limited.

> It has been suggested to me often, and I think myself, that my cartoon 'Tiggy Touchwood' being so popular here, might find equal favour overseas. I like 'Tiggy Touchwood' and would like to make the cartoon a big success, and feel quite confident that I can. I regret therefore that I must give you notice as from this date of closing our agreement, unless you have a more interesting proposal to make me. No. 331 will be my final contribution.

The bald acceptance from the newspaper read:

> We note with regret that you wish to close our agreement relating to the 'Tiggy Touchwood' cartoon and that your final contribution will be No. 331.

May, centre, with Win and Bert Preston in Bowral, 1929.

May and J. O. in Bowral, 1929.

And so by the end of 1931 May Gibbs' drawings disappeared from the Sydney press. The brevity of J. O.'s entries in his diary reflect the tenseness of the situation.

> *October 12* B & B to go out
> Resigned from *Sun*
> *October 22* Joined the New Guard

J. O. reported the news to the family in the West:

> Mamie could not stand the associations of the Sunday Press here and resigned. As a result she found herself barred as far as Sydney, Victorian and West Australian connections were concerned, with a heavy loss in income. The controllers of our Sunday Press are not very nice people!

Despite the air of gloom, it was not the end of the inhabitants of Gumnut Town. May's followers in New Zealand, South Australia and Queensland enjoyed the continuance of the gumnut adventurers.

The *Woman's Budget* and Queensland magazines still printed 'Gumnut Gossip', so although there was a dramatic decline in income, the artist's output continued much the same with one major exception, 'Tiggy Touchwood'. A casualty of May's discontent with newspapers, Tiggy's career ceased at No. 331, but the indestructible little pig was to appear years later as heroine in the last of May's books set in Gumnut Land, *Scotty in Gumnut Land* and *Mr and Mrs Bear and Friends.*

With the greatly reduced income from the cartoons and columns, the sale of May's books once more became an important contributor to earnings. Angus and Robertson had issued paperback versions of all the gumnut books as a means of keeping them alive during the depression and these were selling well.

As the effects of the depression were gradually felt at No. 5 Wallaringa Avenue, May was aware that reductions or cancellations could come with any mail, thereby reducing their income further, but she was reluctant to discuss the matter with her husband who seemed incapable of coping with the worry, let alone making constructive suggestions for dealing with it.

J. O.'s reaction was to place the blame for New South Wales' economic problems squarely on the shoulders of Jack Lang and his socialistic supporters.

It was time to look further afield and possible assistance came in the form of Norman Waterhouse, a relative of Nutcote's designer. When outlining his plans to further his engineering career in the United States, Norman offered to act as May Gibbs' representative in North America. Overtures had been made to the United States market in 1928 but had not been pursued.

As an American release had been the stuff of only their wildest dreams, they were thus more than happy to have such an offer and Norman Waterhouse sailed off for a career in New York as an architect-engineer, with the added responsibility of all May Gibbs' creations.

Inspired by Waterhouse's ingenuity, J. O. suggested that Colonel Percy Kilkelly, a relative in England, might be able to approach British publishers on their behalf.

Nell Palmer, J. O.'s invaluable new assistant, was enterprising enough to unearth boxes of pictures for calendars, a project which had been pushed aside for some years. Acting as May's agent, Nell visited various business houses, disposing of thousands of items for which she received a small commission.

As a reward for her enterprise, the Kellys invited Nell to accompany them on a camping holiday to Canberra. On the trip, Nell was impressed by the fact that Mrs Kelly never seemed to stop work, making copious notes in a pocket book, while drinking interminable cups of tea. The young woman also observed that the elderly couple really seemed to enjoy roughing it and were not inclined to spend heavily on entertainment.

Like all holidays, this one was rejuvenating for the artist and May came back to her drawing board to complete the *Bib and Bub Painting Book* in 1932, which the Nutcote company had decided to produce and market themselves. The reproduction of this painting book is far superior to that of the *Bib and Bub* cartoon books and contains a wealth of fun for young readers with explicit instructions to would-be painters. The initial sales were quite heartening at two shillings each but, unfortunately, business soon tailed off and J. O. became convinced booksellers were trying to block their enterprise.

The new book did bring a call for May Gibbs' other works and Angus and Robertson set up for a new release of *Snugglepot and Cuddlepie, Little Ragged Blossom* and *Little Obelia.* The covers for *Nuttybub and Nittersing* and *Chucklebud and Wunkydoo* were redesigned and included in this release.

Norman Waterhouse's initial letter in November 1931 describing his arrival in New York was full of glowing prospects. Although North America was experiencing a horrific financial crisis, Norman managed to secure a position with a firm of engineering consultants. He then turned his efforts to the publishing houses and later wrote:

> Everyone admired her penmanship and ideas, but nothing practical has come up.

Six months later, he was to send a full report of his efforts. Dodd, Mead and Co., Frederick Stokes, Rand McNally, Reilly Lee, W. H. Barse and Co., Cupples and Son all declined the submissions and Waterhouse explained the situation in a number of letters.

> They like the books, but times are so bad. They do not want to publish any new books in 1932.
>
> *and*
>
> In the US the vast majority of best sellers are cheap juvenile work, that have a large circulation and sell for $1 US, whereas your books could not be published and retail for less than $4 US, twice the price A & R sells for.
>
> *and*
>
> Publishers are astounded at your circulation of 34,000 per book, as books in your class do not reach that circulation.
>
> *and*
>
> I might add the sale of children's books here now is lower than it has ever been in the publishing history of this country, so parents just have not the money to spend on good books for their children.

The final summing up of Norman Waterhouse reflects his disappointment:

> Publishers will not accept foreign talent. Even foreign students are banned now. Mrs Kelly's work, although individuals like it, could really never be placed here. It is a fact it is foreign. Australia's depression is kindergarten compared with here.

Colonel Kilkelly's army training equipped him to confront the British publishing houses and he laid the groundwork by approaching a literary agent, A. P. Watt and Son. Some weeks later a lengthy letter from Kilkelly arrived at Nutcote. Dated March 1932, it explained the agent's appraisal.

> The chief point is that the whole setting of them is in every detail Australian. The birds, animals, trees and other objects around which the stories are written are all Australian. If the donor is confronted with two possible gifts, one with an English setting and the other with an Australian one, I think the choice would always go to the English book ... These five books are quite good of their kind—for Australian children.

A dejected pair in Australia tried to feel cheered by Kilkelly's accompanying remark.

> I feel sure something will come of this and I am not going to be discouraged by 'Watt' like rebuffs. Just keep your pecker up.

The next communication they received was by the new and amazingly speedy airmail service. Unfortunately, it only allowed them to hear the disappointing news earlier. Kilkelly had approached his task in an organised fashion, but found publishers immune.

> It is an astonishingly difficult task to get into the inner sanctum of these publishing fellows, but here's the reports.
>
> Methuen and Co. say they are all right of their kind—except that I believe there is a prejudice among English Editors against naked children, also there are too many artists at work on comic strips.

Roberts of the Incorporated Society of Authors extracted thirty shillings from Kilkelly for May Gibbs' membership and then assessed her work and advised:

> The only possible difficulty I foresee is that the creatures with which the books deal are limited entirely to those to be found in Australia.
> Kilkelly's communications went on:
> Frederick Warne replied, 'Of the five volumes, we like best the illustration for *Snugglepot and Cuddlepie*, but in fact the pictures of animals in the companion volumes are quite amusing. Unfortunately, we do not care for your drawings of babies.' A brusque letter from Blackie and Son, Glasgow said, 'Mothers want very pretty babies.' May's old publisher Harrap rejected the volumes and so did a lot of others.
> In a letter to the parents J. O. recounted Kilkelly's efforts.
> Percy has walked all over London with the Gumnuts. The beasts of publishers in England are too narrow minded to embrace Australia. Somehow I find that the people who adjudicate on what is good literary pabulum for us, or what we need artistically are usually barking up the wrong tree.

> What a kid likes, he very seldom gets a chance to say. It appears to us that the stereotyped fairy with butterfly wings and the dear old fatuous stories appeal to the publishers. Why, they even seem to object to the fact that 'Gumnuts' are unclothed!

J. O. was always a staunch ally. He leapt to May's defence in the wake of criticism and it was he who kept the pair in touch with May's parents in Perth by corresponding regularly with Herbert. It was therefore a hard blow for May during these depressed times when J. O.'s health suddenly declined. A man who thrived with dash in the good times, he was profoundly affected by the depression. His long bouts of silence were interspersed with fiery conversations with Frank de Groot and other New Guardsmen.

The Sydney Harbour Bridge incident, when Frank de Groot illegally rode ahead and slashed the ribbon prior to the official opening, caused consternation throughout Australia and excitement and anxiety certainly took a toll on J. O.'s health. He collapsed with a peptic ulcer and, for several weeks, was seriously ill in hospital. Daily, May and the 'Dodgem' chugged across the now famous bridge to visit the hospital.

Despite her anxiety and the daily hospital visits, May continued to work. Angus and Robertson had requested some Gibbs input to a series of small books they planned and she concentrated on layouts and manuscripts for these, entitled *Babie Days* (sic), *Gardening Days* and *Fishing Days.* She also submitted a book of short stories titled *Tales Old Daddy Tortoise Tells.* Sadly, A & R did not proceed with the series and, after considering the short stories, declined publication.

The greatest asset May had at this time was Nell Palmer. A bright personality, she was willing also to turn her hand to household chores as well as office duties and so earned a special place at Nutcote.

May looked forward to Nell's daily reports of the Palmer household of father, mother and their children and Nell's stories provided a fund of ideas for the artist. Soon the bandicoot family started to reflect the comings and goings of the Palmer household.

After the success of Nell Palmer's calendar sales in 1932, May voiced her thoughts aloud to Nell that perhaps the *Sunday Sun* might again be interested in 'Bib and Bub' and Nell took the artist up on the veiled request and offered to storm the editor's room to face Eric Baume.

When granted an interview, Nell calmly presented her proposal, carefully pointing out that New South Wales children—and adults—were being denied 'Bib and Bub', while other states were enjoying the strip. Even as she spoke, she was aware that Eric Baume was finding it difficult to disguise his delight with the gumnut comic strip as it lay on his desk.

During the conversation, Sir Errol Knox entered the room and, scooping up one of the strips, laughed heartily at its content and started down memory lane, relating how Mrs Kelly came to him with the first gumnut cartoon strip. Baume informed him that May Gibbs was looking for a Sydney paper and Sir Errol's delight encouraged Baume to welcome the gumnuts back. Baume agreed, however he added that although he had always liked 'Bib and Bub', he did not like dealing with Mrs Kelly and would only have the strip back provided he did not have to deal with her personally.

Although obviously delighted with the success of Nell's venture, May was apparently hurt by Baume's remarks. When she mentioned casually, 'You can look after the deliveries to Baume', it was the first time Nell had heard May refer to anyone by a bold surname. She felt that May Gibbs could be an unforgiving opponent.

On 25 June 1933 'Bib and Bub' reappeared in the *Sunday Sun*. Ironically, May Gibbs' comic strip replaced a strip by her young champion of a decade earlier, Syd Nicholls. The cartoon strip 'Us Fellers' was the casualty, but years later Syd was to state:

> If 'Us Fellers' was to be replaced by anything I preferred May Gibbs' 'Bib and Bub' to anything else. Mrs Kelly did valuable work for the children of Australia.

A generous compliment from one of Australia's great cartoonists.

Herbert and Cecilia's last visit to Nutcote had been in 1929 and Cecie was now not well enough to allow the pioneer couple to undertake any more lengthy journeys. In fact, for the past few years, Cecie's health had been causing considerable concern. So, four years later, when both May and J. O. felt the need for a respite from Nutcote, they returned once more to the West, sailing on the *Manunda*, a well known interstate passenger ship.

'The Gibbs of Perth' in 1933. Back row, left to right: *Ivan, J. O.* Front row, left to right: *Josephine, baby John, Elizabeth, Cecilia, Ken, May, Herbert.*

With the responsibility of keeping up a supply of 'Bib and Bub' and 'Gumnut Gossip', the holiday was not an escape from work for May but it did give her a change of location from her studio.

It was time for a grand reunion. Gathered in Perth with Herbert and Cecilia were Ivan and his wife, Josephine, with their three children, Elizabeth, Kenneth and John, and the ever-faithful Calanchini.

As usual, May did not want any fuss. She kept to her immediate family, and under the shady trees in the garden of The Dune, spent long hours talking with her father and cousin Marjorie. She also spent many hours in her father's studio, for deadlines had to be met.

When Cali offered May his automobile to tour the countryside, the Kellys were delighted to drive out in the bush again and together they rediscovered the beauties of southern Western Australia. The storyteller was greeted by the biggest and most beautiful gumnuts and blossoms of Australia and a radiant display of the wildflowers her tales had made famous. Those tales had opened the eyes of human beings—particularly young human beings—to the Australian forest.

May recalled a sense of affinity with the Australian bush that was even more powerful in the West. She delighted in the observation of a reviewer:

> May Gibbs stuck her tiny roots into the soil with a grip that is reflected in her work.

When it was time to return to the East, May took a long farewell of her parents, both of whom were becoming noticeably frailer. She stood at the carriage window waving a wattle-yellow scarf. It was to be their final parting.

16

BUSINESS AS USUAL

Well, Kid, it's some cloud and the little cartoon job gets the minimum of attention.

Letter to Rene Sullivan

By 1935 newspaper management was in the hands of a new breed of editors, who, dominated by deadlines, seemed quite unsympathetic to the problems of creative contributors. It was an era of syndication of overseas material, particularly American strips, and Australian cartoonists were fighting an uphill battle for space against the inclusion of such luminaries as 'Speed Gordon', 'Mandrake', 'Mickey Mouse', 'Tim Tyler' and 'Father', of *Bringing Up Father* fame. May had constant concern over the renewal of contracts, except in Queensland where her publishers had never hinted at decreased fees, diminished space or discontinuing her works.

Australia's highest paid cartoonist was, at this time, Jim Bancks who was rumoured to receive £40 to £50 per week for his popular cartoon strip, 'Ginger Meggs'. May Gibbs' £5 5s seemed paltry in comparison. J. O. could, understandably, not accept the inequality. He believed 'Bib and Bub' was held in insufficient esteem by male editors, who possibly related their childhood experiences to the 'Ginger Meggs' adventures. His contempt for the publishing world was relayed to anyone who came within earshot and recorded in letters to the family and friends, as in this outburst to his brother-in-law:

> You have a father and sister and I have a father-in-law and wife, two very unusual people, infinitely more ornamental and useful to the world than you and I. They are both undervalued.
>
> One is buried as an Under-Secretary of Lands; now any intelligent lad could, by dint of running consciously along between the lines in a rut, in due course attain that position.
>
> The other spends her days and her brilliant talent for 'pure line', doing amusing drawings, which delight thousands, but still she is at the beck and call of illiterate, ignorant Advertising managers (who, nowadays, control newspapers).
>
> Her graceful drawing, her fertile fancy are paid at the same rate as a junior in a bank.

May herself was far more immediately hurt by rejections, cancellations and criticism, as in the following letter from a publisher in her home state.

> You will notice that sketches for children now appearing in the *Western Mail* are not as juvenile as those compounded by Miss Gibbs. For these reasons I return your submissions with thanks.

And though prepared to defend herself May recognised that this was one battle she might not win. A New Zealand paper's wish to reduce her fee brought this response.

> As for quality, I would like to point out that I am the only feature Artist exploiting purely Australasian matter and fauna. I have maintained this style of work as I feel the children of Australasia should have the opportunity of becoming familiar with their own animals. I do appreciate that cheap foreign syndicating is making the position of the Australian Artist very difficult and my epilogue.

They were troubled times. May was finding that the work did not flow as smoothly as it once had and she was aware of pressure to deliver her material on time. This stress was further aggravated by a fall, which led to a noticeable deterioration in her health. Gradually she found herself less equal to maintaining deadlines—and to handling the inevitable confrontations with editors this would provoke.

One of her favourite editors was Connie Robertson of the *Woman's Budget,* a lady who delighted in the gumnuts and who could remain gracious even when chiding May for late delivery. On her departure from the publication, she was replaced by Vera Hamilton, who in a forthright manner established that she had little time for the gumnuts. May subsequently felt the subject of a barrage of criticism, culminating in the following letter, dated 23 October 1935.

> It appears that practically all your subjects are far too advanced for the children of the age which they are expected to entertain. For instance, I dislike intensely any allusion to racing and betting for small children. I find too that your copy is full of mispronounced words.
>
> Serpently (certainly)
> Persurdity (absurdity)
> Sumpin (something)
> Persackerley (exactly)

> I do not think that such pronunciations are good for children and they are difficult to unlearn as is baby talk.
>
> It contains too many one line sentences.
>
> Would you please not exceed 850 words in your copy and make your animals talk like ordinary human beings (but with minds attuned to children's joys and sorrows and not adult entertainments such as races and grown-up drawing room parties).
>
> Could not your characters be boy and girl animals, rather than men and women?

May could rarely take advice and certainly not the advice handed out by one of her favourite characters to his contemporaries. 'Old Bill' always advised antagonists to 'say nuthin' but, unfortunately, his creator was in no mood for such advice.

> I think that you are in error when you allude to 'mispronunciations'. Inventing humorous perversions of words is not mis-pronouncing.
>
> If I cannot have your assurance that there will be no further mutilation of my words, I shall be compelled to withdraw the contribution, as I cannot have the standard of my work lowered.

The written battle between Nutcote and the *Woman's Budget* culminated in May's resignation.

May, despite her authorial talent for perverse pronunciations, spoke the most correct English. Unlike some educationalists of the period, she also knew children play at being adults and particularly play at being someone who had captured their admiration or imagination. She never talked down to her readers, but involved them by introducing real life situations and settings to her fantasy. Australian children, to the 'Mother of the Gumnuts', were unlike any other children in the world.

> They are a distinct type, are brighter, more intelligent, possess a greater ingenuity; are able to speak and think for themselves, and they begin to show their independence very early. I have a wealth of correspondence which reveals they relate to my works.

Unexpectedly, Eric Baume, who at that time had become responsible for the *Woman's Budget* as well as the *Sunday Sun*, was distressed by May's resignation and asked her to revive 'Tiggy' for the *Budget.* In a reversal of form, however, J. O. replied with a firm 'No!' to the offer. He explained his actions to the family in the following letter.

> I say NO! She's had quite enough of it. A heavy strain, more than most people can grasp and leading eventually to a breakdown. Doesn't it seem rough Gub [Herbert], that Mamie should be in a perpetual cat fight literally for her artistic existence.

Life at Nutcote had now become one of routine, of gardening and work interrupted by visitors. Some of J. O.'s time was occupied with correspondence with Angus and Robertson who had allowed May's titles to go out of stock without reprinting. Writing home to Perth he informs of

> ... the offensive against A & R who admit all Mamie's work is out of print. Isn't it rotten. They are to see Mamie beginning of week, and arrange something. They say there is a *demand* from customers for her work.

> A further shot at A & R was on 16 November 1935:
> A & R have broken faith again, notwithstanding their written guarantee to produce, at latest, early in October, the books are not on the counter yet.

Angus and Robertson managed republication by Christmas and the record of J. O.'s 'offensive' ends with that report.

May had a number of negotiations with Angus and Robertson during the latter part of 1935. The one and only attempt she made at publishing her own work had proved a failure. This was the *Bib and Bub Painting Book,* published in 1932. With the artist finally in a position to control every aspect of its production, it was a very high quality, beautifully presented book. But, as a result, it was very expensive in relation to similar material available. J. O.'s despair of the venture is recalled in his letters.

> Also I got all the Painting books left, some 2,600 of them. A & R say confidently they can make a bulk sale for 4d. As we need the money and can't sell them I'm just as glad to cut our loss before the silver fish do [it] for us.

There was unexpected excitement in the mid-thirties. The Australian Broadcasting Commission arranged to adapt *Tales of Snugglepot and Cuddlepie* for radio. The program was a great success and also resulted in a rush on May Gibbs' books, for which Angus and Robertson were unprepared. A happier outcome for May and J. O. was the pile of mail which arrived at No. 5 Wallaringa Avenue. It lifted their spirits if not their bank balance.

Inevitably, the success of this venture called for a celebration holiday and the couple were off on another camping trip, heading for the trout streams of the southeast. The bush was still their haven, and while May recorded the journey in her sketch book, J. O. reported to the family.

> We did some 1700 miles during our Safari, camping and wearing our shabbiest kit and were out seven weeks.
>
> Most inexpensive and jolly and certainly healthy. The old bus stood up to her work splendidly. We averaged 21 mpg, which is pretty good for a very heavily loaded car over indifferent and hilly roads, some rather nerve racking. Mamie nursed the dear old Dodgibusteribus most fondly.

On their return, there were further indications that their fortunes were improving when approaches were made regarding an animated film of 'Bib and Bub'. A Miss Dorothy Brown had requested permission to represent May Gibbs in placing the gumnuts with American and British studios. May's solicitor, Henry Wilson of Roxburgh and Co., was enthusiastic about the project and busied himself with contracts. The Kellys had always been interested in the Walt Disney animations and many discussions had already taken place regarding the gumnuts' suitability to animation. As an artist May was aware of the thousands of work hours required on such a project and she seemed over-awed at the prospect of this tremendous concentration on her characters.

May worked feverishly to get her newspaper commitments completed in advance, so that she would be available for any demands of the new project. However, the waiting stretched on and on until it eventually became obvious that their dreams were not to be realised. It was a bitter disappointment.

May turned her attention to the Scotties and the dogs became her main hobby. Both the Kellys had tremendous pride in their 'family' and May would never part with one of them until she had thoroughly investigated its future home and owners, even delivering the puppies personally so she could verify their worthiness.

While May occupied herself with her work, the dogs and the garden, J. O. was finding it much more difficult to be optimistic and gradually slumped again into a state of depression. Accustomed to his extremes of mood, May hardly noticed his decline but, when he suddenly suffered a severe heart attack, she was aware that he was an old man. Recurring attacks were to reduce him to a permanent invalid. Although now in her sixties, May was still extremely active, but was finding it difficult to keep up her weekly comic strip while she nursed J. O. and coped with housework, the Scotties and the garden.

Following a merger of the *Sunday Sun* and *Sun-Herald*, a new 'Bib and Bub' contract had to be drawn up and the editor, Mr F. W. Tonkin, did not look forward to the meeting he had scheduled with the difficult Mrs Kelly, whose volatile behaviour with editors was by now legendary. When a tiny figure, huddled in her well-worn fur coat, sat opposite his desk and sadly stated in her beautiful English voice, 'But we can't survive on £5 5s,' Mr Tonkin heard himself offering her £6 6d per strip. This was the sum the most prolific artist in Australia's cartoon history was to receive for the rest of the strip's newspaper life. The only change to this fee occurred when Australia changed to decimal currency in 1966. The £6 6s was converted into $13.65.

By the year 1938, when the worst of the depression was over, the world was again threatened by a possible global war. A greater blow for May, however, was the news that Herbert was seriously ill and, for the first time, she admitted to feeling old. With their dwindling fortune and ill health, it was a time of sadness and low spirits. Amongst her notes, May jotted:

> The artist who died of drawing gumnuts while she wanted to draw clouds.

Despite his own problems, J. O. expressed his concern about May to her family.

> I am very worried about Mamie. She is mentally dead beat. Year in and year out she has not let up for a holiday. No theatres or pictures or relaxation of any sort.

The Kellys now had few visitors and became steadily more isolated. Seated in a dentist's waiting room, May wrote to the person who understood her best.

> My Darling Rene,
>
> Just read your last letter and you aren't the only one at the dentist's. I am ringing up a big bill now.
>
> J. O. is still sick, he had two very bad days, pain in the chest, lying down and sleeping fitfully, irritable and flying off one night because I washed the kitchen floor after washing up, made himself

> worse off of course and I nearly beside myself inwardly, can't scold have to be so careful.
>
> I felt all crushed and suffocated.
>
> Well, Kid, it's some cloud and the little cartoon job gets the minimum of attention.
>
> I feel I must give J. O. proper food, but am a bad hand as you know.
>
> Does it seem that fate gives with one hand and spanks you with another?

Rene had retired from the postal service some years earlier after Joe had died and was quick to respond to May's letter. It took only a day or so to pack and make the necessary arrangements, then she turned the key in her little rented cottage at Laurieton and caught the train to Sydney.

May was naturally delighted at Rene's arrival. Although J. O. maintained crustily that she was not a good cook, the old political adversaries called a truce and Rene stayed to nurse him for many months.

James Ossoli Kelly died in August 1939, just prior to the outbreak of the Second World War.

May Gibbs never spoke of her sorrow, in fact she rarely discussed her husband of over twenty years. However, shortly before her death, she made the comment.

> He and I were such tremendous pals. Always immaculately dressed, quite unconscious of himself, beautifully spoken and friends with everybody. He encouraged me tremendously in my work.

The day of J. O.'s death, Eric Marden, the gardener who had often shared a joke with J. O., suggested to Mrs Kelly that, as a sign of respect, he would not come the following day, and was more than a little surprised when she replied, 'Oh yes, oh yes, Eric, business as usual', and swung off down the path, adjusting her gardening gloves.

Business was not quite as usual for May, who now had to rely more on her solicitor's help. But not all matters were referred thence as the following draft letter indicates. It provides, as well, a cheerful reminder of May's ebullience. There is no record of a reply from the AMP so possibly this arrantly charming epistle was never posted.

The Manager
AMP Society
29 June, 1940
Dear Sir,

After apology for delay in replying to your letter of 13 June, 1940 in which you inform of a raise in my mortgage rate, I am, I'm afraid, going to plead guilty with you.

First, I'm not a Business woman and I can't even spell nor can I count the change when out shopping!

I am just a mere comic person. I earn my living, that is, by being a comic, at least I try to be comic in my cartoons every Sunday in the children's page of the *Sunday Sun*. Perhaps when you were a little boy you read them!!

Now to get right down to tintacks. Why must you raise my interest from $4\frac{1}{2}$ to $5\frac{1}{4}$ on The Mortgage? (I'm sorry that's wrong.) I mean from $4\frac{1}{2}$ to $5\frac{1}{2}$. Can you have the heart when I tell you I haven't had a new hat in 3 years!

If you could only see the patched undies hanging on my clothes-line! But quite apart from such pathetic details let me beg you to consider taxation soaring goodness knows where, rise in household costs, appeals for every kind fund which of course must be honoured. Consider the chance one takes with books. Royalties are cut, people won't publish, 'Pig won't get over the style and ...', oh, I beg your pardon! I really can't write a Business letter and I hope this doesn't come in one of your bad moments when everything goes wrong and your office staff is trembling.

Back to tintacks.

Please don't put up my rate of interest. My property is a valuable one, in good order and very sound—so is my money, always paid promptly and with a smile.

Won't you persuade yourself to think again and think in terms of $4\frac{1}{2}$? it would be so easy for me as after 6 years of practice it is quite a habit.

If I have caught you in a bad moment and there are so many about these days, please accept my sincere apologies.

I am
Very Faithfully yours
C.M. Ossoli Kelly
(May Gibbs)

May was now sixty-two. Her working hours were occupied by 'Bib and Bub' and the rest of the day was devoted to her garden and the Scotty dogs. Save for long visits by Rene from Laurieton and Eric's regular attendance to the garden May spent considerable time by herself and complained of her loneliness to her solicitor and friend Henry Wilson. His practical solution was to organise a tenant to occupy her downstairs rooms. Thereafter a succession of people shared the Nutcote address and provided May with company when needed and sometimes with friendships which endured beyond the tenancy.

In all their twenty years of marriage J. O. had been a regular correspondent with Herbert and thus kept May's family in touch with her life 'totherside'. After J. O.'s death, May took over the role herself and received in return regular reports from home. May preserved her father's letters which reveal, besides a loving relationship, something of the enormous influence Herbert had on his daughter. The gentle teacher and mentor encouraged his student to look and observe even the smallest of details.

31 August 1940

My darling May,

... You probably remember the little gum tree, the only one left of the clump near the little balcony? I have several times found this clever copy of the gumnut on dead boughs from the top of the tree but could never find one on a live branch, I think the little builders must be inhabitants of the tree tops, and that they are some sort of wasp or bee, something like the little insect which cuts pieces out of the rose leaves to line their nests on the ground, they have pieces of various shapes for the ends and for the completion of the little nest ...

... I am longing to sit quietly and watch and listen to country birds (instead of town doves with their call of—according to Cali—'The Castor oil quick') and the rivers—I wonder what fish they have in them.

Dearest love
Father

Written in a very shaky hand, this was to be Herbert's last letter to his daughter. On 4 October Herbert Gibbs died. Considering the distance which had separated them for so many years, the loss came as a tremendous blow, one which May described as the greatest sadness in her life, and one from which she took a long time to recover. In her notebook, the only comment she made was:

To think much is to be sad
To think more is to be calm.

On 26 March 1941, just five months after Herbert had preceded her on his last journey, Cecie followed.

May in Vaucluse, 1937.

17
SCOTTIES, BEARS AND A DANDE LION

I used to walk about the garden, weeding it and loving it, with a book in my pocket and a pencil and that's where I got my best ideas ...

May Gibbs interview

Australia facing its enemies of the early forties was a more vibrant nation than the Australia of the depression. Although the population had to make sacrifices, a common bond gave them a new strength.

During the forties, May's cartoons were inspired with a wealth of ideas stimulated by people in action, and Bib and Bub, together with the inhabitants of Gumnut Land, found themselves in situations which mirrored the problems of all Australians—rationing, lack of petrol, air raid sirens, wardens and the home guard all were subjects for her strip. The cartoons from this period are among some of her cleverest work, as her puckish sense of humour made lighthearted comment on the inconveniences of the war period.

The war and consequent shortage of materials limited the availability of good paper and all printed works were produced on paper of an inferior quality. Three of the May Gibbs classics, *Tales of Snugglepot and Cuddlepie, Little Ragged Blossom* and *Little Obelia* were presented as one book and titled *The Complete Adventures of Snugglepot and Cuddlepie.* The author apologised to her readers for the quality of the production.

Dear Everybody,

Our pictures were not printed in a fog or a sandstorm. It's the war. Nobody could get us the right paper. But our story is just the same.

Signed
Snugglepot and Cuddlepie.

The quality of this book was to be upgraded in later years but unfortunately the books were never returned to their original form.

The war also brought a new demand for Australian material and, encouraged by Rene, May decided to write a new book. The loss of one of the Scotty dogs from the Nutcote compound triggered off the idea.

Scotty in Gumnut Land, published in 1941, is May Gibbs at her storytelling best. She takes all her favourite characters and weaves them about her leading man, Scotty. Most of her readers had a favourite amongst her characters, so everyone in Gumnut Land was included in the adventure.

May's delightful preparatory notes for *Scotty in Gumnut Land* reveal the artist's method of approach—a confident attack on the illustration while the plot is left to thicken.

> 'Notes for Scotty—Cover: strong blacks (Scotty), green and pink (gumnuts and leaves), one good frontispiece in 3 colours. Characters: Scotty, Dr Stork, Tiggy Touchwood. (Could she come as nurse, late in story and save an awful situation?) Bad Banksiamen with cart and bags—gathers animals and takes them to badness knows where ...

The popularity of the 'Bib and Bub' cartoon, which often featured Mr and Mrs Scotty and family, ensured the book's success. May dedicated the book to her audience, as well as her only niece and two nephews.

> To all Children who love and try to understand Animals, and Birds, and small Creatures. (May they learn to see the unfairness, and unloveliness, of caged wings.) And to Elizabeth and Ken and John Gibbs, in particular, I dedicate this story.
>
> With love,
> May Gibbs.

In some of the illustrations for *Scotty in Gumnut Land*, May used a format which had won for her her first art competition as a twelve-year-old. Included in the overall composition of some of the drawings are smaller pictures which illustrate the progressive adventures of the hero of the story.

Scotty in Gumnut Land, priced at 4s 6d, was very successful and, with the release of *The Complete Adventures of Snugglepot and Cuddlepie*, produced yearly sales that reminded the publishers of May Gibbs' successes of the twenties.

By teaching children to love the bush and its creatures, May had always conveyed her keen concern for animals in the most effective way. Her strongest appeal on their behalf was made when *Mr and Mrs Bear and Friends* was released in November 1943 and set out guidelines to young readers on how to communicate with their pets and wildlife. This sequel to *Scotty in Gumnut Land*, her last book set in the bush world of Gumnut Land, is unlike her previous story books in that it does not carry a dedication. In it she also continued the story of Miffrend, the kindly human whose reclusive existence and entourage of Scotty dogs mirrored what was becoming May's own preferred lifestyle.

Still searching for new challenges, May experimented with writing adult fiction. Four short stories titled *Spotlights on George and Mrs George and Kitty's Ankles, Old Clothes, Very Little Small Old Book,* and *The Pink Pearl* were submitted to *Life Digest* who were interested in the collection. Negotiations proceeded but May refused to have the books published under her own name. Naturally, the publishers wanted the May Gibbs name, because there was a ready market for her work, but the author remained adamant and the stories remained unpublished. May then attempted a mystery story, to be called *The Man Across the Road*, but she soon tired of its construction and retreated into the bush world she had created.

As soon as the war was over and petrol became easier to obtain, May instructed Eric to go over the 'Dodgem' so it would be in working order to take to the road again. She had missed her trips to the bush and she needed new ideas to get away from the war-time themes. The old chariot made a few valiant efforts to do the journeys of yesteryear but soon found itself confined to weekly shopping expeditions to Neutral Bay. For these, the 'Dodgem', with Mrs Kelly at the wheel, companions and yapping dogs seated in strategic positions, would follow a cleverly designed course. By taking a certain route, only left hand turns had to be made, thus enabling the pilot to negotiate the journey with a minimum of fuss. It was a sight to delight the locals who regretted the eventual swapping of the old bus for a tiny black Austin, which was nicknamed the 'Tar-baby' because, as May confided to a friend, 'Like the Tar-baby in Brer Rabbit he mostly just sits.'

The early fifties saw the passing of May's young brother, Harold, her cousin Win Preston and the faithful Calanchini, but the greatest loss was the death of Rene, who died of cancer.

May was left very much alone and her misery was revealed in the lines scribbled next to one of her working drawings of the period.

There seems a throb in this life of ours
A great throb of pain
And though I miss its beat for hours
It surely comes again.

There seems a cry in every heart
A simple cry within
And would to heaven I could part
My weary self from sin.

There is then comfort in the thought
Of others who like me
Seem rarely doing what they ought
This move through misery.

The comic strip met its deadlines but as her relative Mabel King maintained, 'May wasn't herself' after Rene's death.

And now indeed the 'Tar-baby' mostly just sat. The period of May's trips to the bush was at an end. Gradually, as she kept more and more to her home, the garden became her main source of inspiration until finally it was her only source. For the last eighteen years of her life May left her home and garden only when driven by illness.

On the edge of Neutral Bay, the little house of May Gibbs was a landmark for those riding the ferry to Kurraba Wharf and often they would catch a glimpse of its owner. May would wear an enormous hat, cleverly provided with a hole in the brim so that she might peep out unobserved and watch the passers-by.

'People who keep untidy back yards must have untidy back minds', she had once jotted in a notebook. More than anything, May loved her garden and would be out in it every day, and, to one trained to observe the smallest detail, it was a rich source of inspiration. In an interview for the Australian Archives, she explained her approach to work:

> I used to walk about the garden, weeding it and loving it, with a book in my pocket and a pencil and that's where I got my best ideas; out in the open, gardening. I'd write a note of them, then I'd go in with a wet towel on my head, right up into the far reaches of the night, and do the work, and everyone else would be in bed sleeping and I wouldn't have any interruptions, you see.

It is not surprising then that in the last book May Gibbs was to write the garden was the source of her fantasy world. Titled *Prince Dande Lion ... A Garden Whim Wham,* May described it as one 'For older children, and I hope, some quite old ones'.

The book was a departure from May's usual style and in it she indulged her passion for puns. The King rode a horse called Radish, the Queen rode Adendron, Prince Dande Lion's mount was the ass, Pidistra, and his dog a Poinsettia, '... a sorter red settia dog that points at things'. Panthus spring out from the trees—'... aga panthus ... terrible savage they be'.

People become ageratum, they go through doors marked 'Privat', cyclists are cyclamen, the maid announces, 'Miss Em Byranthe, Mum', the characters suffer from plumbago and sail from Port Ulaca.

A reader with a knowledge of flowers and a delight in punning could find pleasure in translating May Gibbs' play on words. For the less informed, the book included a 'salpiglossary'.

The book was first submitted to Angus and Robertson in 1951 and accepted for publication. Managing editor Beatrice Davis conveyed to May the company's pleasure in having a new May Gibbs title but their reservations about the extensive use of punning. She suggested reducing this. May, however, while politely thanking A & R for their 'valuable suggestions', ignored them all. Undeterred, A & R made preparations for publication but almost two years had passed when the following was sent by The Firm.

> As the cost of producing *Prince Dande Lion* would still be more than the public would pay, I suggest we hold this title until it can be published successfully.

May was apparently unprepared to wait and later that same year, 1953, Ure Smith released *Prince Dande Lion.*

As with all her books May suffered the usual waiting pains and doubts as her notes to herself at this time reveal.

> Memo for matters to talk about with Mr Horton.
> 1 Copyright in America.
> 2 Can the Bookshops be told when to expect 'Dandy'. They don't even know there is a new M.G. book. Dymocks, A & R, Bookshop in Mosman.
> 3 Price?
> 4 Exactly how far is it ready? I feel it is being held back.

Ure Smith had it out for Christmas but it was to prove a sad failure when first published. The author had the humiliating experience of watching the price of *Prince Dande Lion* gradually slide from 14s 9d to 9s 6d then to 3s before it was eventually remaindered.

When the *Northern Queensland Register*, with nearly thirty years' association her most faithful newspaper publisher, requested a different size format for 'Bib and Bub', May Gibbs resigned from the paper. The editor wrote expressing his feelings:

> We are sorry indeed to have your note terminating the commission to the *Northern Queensland Register*.
>
> Through 'Bib and Bub', we have had a close association of interests and, although you may not recall, it was I who arranged with you in Sydney, for that wonderful weekly feature for our newspaper.
>
> So many people, now grown-ups, call and refer to the Gumnuts feature of their younger days.
>
> [Signed Ellis]

As usual, May had acted without sufficient thought and though touched by the editor's remarks, she refused to go back on her decision.

But there was still 'Bib and Bub' to send off weekly to the *Sun-Herald* and there was still her garden. Most often these were company enough.

My Garden

Though clouds may sail across the blue
My sun is never low
My grapes hang ripe the whole year round
While snowdrops spread like snow.

Far into my sweet garden
All sorts of people stray
And I would like each one of them
To never go away.

But time, my dear old Gardener
Does sternly shake his head

He says 'Some pluck my flowers
And trample many a bed.'

They break my walls and hedges down
That took so long to train
And though he turns them out,
I often let them in again.

Who would not climb on Higher Ground
To gain a better view?
The wish is with the many
The strength is with the few.

There seems a Certain Balance
About the Universe
If you can walk — you walk alone
You may not have a nurse.

The sweetness of the meat
Does show, the nearness of the Bone
A mind may climb the highest tops
To Find Itself Alone!

18

VERY MUCH ALIVE

So you see I am alive with lots of laughter to it.
May Gibbs letter

> You wondered if I were still alive [wrote May in response to a newspaper article of the mid-fifties], VERY MUCH ALIVE, my dear. I'm still working for my living, doing everything in the house (well, a stray few hours of help occasionally) work in the garden, five dogs to care for (little devils they are), myself to cook for, feed and wait upon (big devil I am), visitors—not many, no time—telephone to answer, my secretary (old, like me) to argue with, all business to run, the gardener to supervise, and water-board men, gas men, plumbers, painters, fence menders, electricians—and all this goes to looking after one old woman (me) and an old house. So you see, I am alive—with lots of laughter to it.

And, as those who remember her in her later years recall, there was indeed always much laughter in her life. Though she became more and more reclusive May remained intensely interested in the outside world. She read widely, enjoyed her television set, long telephone conversations and visits from friends once they had established who they were, for often bouts of shyness combined with a great need for privacy brought out the old gift for mimicry as a protective barrier. From behind the firmly closed front door she would growl, 'Mrs Kelly is not at home', and on the telephone would use a falsetto to inform callers, 'No, no Mrs Kelly ain't here.' When those in the know challenged these pronouncements May would laugh sheepishly and chat happily for hours.

And, though wary on first encounter May was quick to make new friendships. When one of Uncle George's granddaughters, Marian, came to Sydney to live she sought out her mother's favourite storyteller, 'Cousin May'.

May tells of their first encounter, revealing both her initial reserve and the open-heartedness which was to result in a lasting and loving friendship with Marian and later her young family.

'Nutcote'
5 Wallaringa Avenue
Neutral Bay

My Dear Little Cos,

What about Xmas Day—have you a nice Xmas Dinner waiting to be engulfed; or have you not quite decided?

You know when you came to see me last—I was *dreadful*!

You looked quite shocked when I said 'I haven't a thing to eat in the house' or words to that effect. Afterwards in the middle of the night I woke and saw your sweet face with that look and I laughed and laughed—I remember all the conversation on my side—How I looked at you almost fiercely and asked in stern tones 'Do you know how many ... live in King's Cross?' You looked so surprised and a little disconcerted! After that I rolled back the years and told you all about an old sore misunderstanding with some very honoured relatives!!! 'Silly isn't it?' said poor little Cousin, face full of embarrassment! Well I had a great midnight laugh and asked myself 'What on earth was the matter with you?' I can only think I was under a spell of bad liver—always a weak point with meself. There was *plenty* of food and I would have loved you to eat any of it and *don't* you bring *anything* to eat my lass, I keep a stock in case of an interesting visitor (the uninteresting ones don't get asked 'to eat') Well now—what weather—it's raining Cats, Dogs and Elephants, and my garden top soil is rushing down into the harbour.

If you want to eat a Picnic, sort of Xmas Dinner, in 'Nutcote'; and if you want to sleep and rest here anytime; then, or earlier or later, I shall be delighted to have you—but do not be the least upsided about it if you have plans made—I want to be useful and I'd love to have you but it will be very quiet; one old, old, not so old friend, not such a friend (there's a difference between FRIEND and FRIEND or friend)—you see what I mean? She is always here to Xmas and seldom any one else these days—she lives just round the corner and is mostly doing nursing at the Old People Rest Homes sort of Hospitals.

Has Robin faded out? Yes, no? Hope you're not too busy these humid days.

Darling, enclosed is my Xmas card to you—a small one, but at least not so inconvenient as a card or a book, or wot not? Buy a bit of chewing gum?

Hoping to see you soon—I have in the House quite a dump of Xmas Cheer that needs nibbling, do come.

Lots of love dear,
Your old new friend
C. M. Ossoli Kelly

In a letter to Win Preston decades earlier May had stated: It has been such a blessing all my life to realise that the unexpected always happens—as I greatly love a surprise.

The surprise which gave May one of the greatest pleasures of her life was to receive an MBE in acknowledgement of her contribution to children's literature. On 9 June 1955, Cecilia May Ossoli Kelly was appointed an ordinary Member of the Most Excellent Order of the British Empire (Civil Division) and the following April, May was invited to Government House for the investiture. By now, she very rarely ventured from the little house at Neutral Bay and, when Eric offered to drive her over to Government House, she declined, explaining her car would not be comfortable amongst the other grand affairs. Eventually, the document and medal were posted to her and the medal in its official case was thereafter kept on a table in her sitting room to be shown with shy pride to rare approved visitors.

May was nearing eighty yet still 'Bib and Bub' arrived on time each week at the *Sun-Herald* and still she was trying something new—another book, as the following letter to Beatrice Davis reveals amongst the reminiscences.

23 January 1956

Dear Beatrice,

Forgive the big gap between Christmas with your charming card and good wishes and the acknowledgement and all my sincere good wishes to you for your 1956. In your work, in your play and in your health.

My dear, I have hunted amongst years of old documents, letters and such, with very often lovely folders nicely titled *but* with quite the wrong stuff inside!!! Somebody appears to have been hunting there before me and messed it all up.

Rather sad work—old letters; Mr Shenstone, Mr Cousins, and even friendly notes from George Robertson himself, and lots, lots and lots of my husband's notes, letters and documentising. I hardly realised what a lot of business went with my work!

Well dear I found *no* copies of contracts—they must either be with my lawyer or stored in the Bank.

Anyway I feel sure we neglected to make a contract for *Scotty in G. Land.* My husband not being here to see to it we probably let it pass.

Could you have one made in line with *Mr & Mrs Bear*—it's the same sort of book?

Xmas and the humid weather 'did me under' and I am going slow on a new book.

Yes I think the new edition of *Scotty* looks well and I hope he'll go well.

If you sell *Dandy* in your House, do see that he is *not* put in with books for the very little. It is really written for older children. I hope you like *Dandy* a little—I should be so disappointed if you did not.

With lots of sincere best wishes
Sincerely
C. M. Ossoli Kelly

The 'new book' was possibly her autobiography. With Marian now a regular visitor, the second cousins spent long hours talking about their relatives and old times at The Harvey. The conversations prompted the author's memory and her interest in writing her life story which she was going to title '*This Other Fair(y) Tale*' by Ann Onymous. She could rarely be persuaded to resist a pun. Among her possessions were scraps of paper with jottings of her early recollections, many of which have been quoted in this book, and she made a number of attempts to start her own story but the effort of gathering the information was beyond her. Exhausted with the task, she wrote the project off as: 'A Muddle of Memories, A Huddle of Hearsay, A Gabble of Gossip, A Riot of Richness'.

May wrote of herself during this time.

She scratched all day on paper white
And half the night scratched she
For she was a student with all her might
A humble student you see.

And she was ancient and aged and worn
And mad as mad could be

So she scratched the ink through dark till dawn
For she was a student you see.

And piles and piles of paper white
With pen and ink spoiled she
When people called she still sat tight
She didn't know you see.

And when she heard who'd been and gone
She tore her hair with woe
It made her look more aged and worn
For she hadn't much you know.

One day in April 1962, one of the Scotty dogs waddled across its owner's path, and the resulting collision left May in a comical, but painful pose. After assuring herself the dog was not injured, the girl from the bush gave the Australian 'Cooee' and was found waiting calmly with a fractured leg.

After an operation when a Smith Peterson pin and plate were inserted, the author set about catching up on her cartoon strip as the thirteen-week advance supply had dwindled during her illness. Never at a loss to use an experience in her life, the stay at the Royal North Shore Hospital provided new material for her Gumnut Land friends. Now relying on a crutch for mobility, May also used her new support as a theatrical prop, brandishing it at the Scotties, Eric and any of her friends who were brave enough to debate a subject with her.

An endeavour was made to record a series of programmes of May reading her stories, and a simple take was put together by her friends. Her fine voice brings the gumnut adventures alive in a charming manner, but unfortunately, she was not up to the physical strain of making a professional recording.

A slight stroke in 1966 brought the eternal fighter out in Mrs Kelly and she spent days practising her signatures, Cecilia May O'Kelly and May Gibbs, with instructions to herself:

> 'I'll keep my wits about me—smart and brittle till I'm fit again.'

Months passed and an older Mrs Kelly tried to match the pace of the young May Gibbs but failed. Her humour never failed her, however, and she was still able to comment on her situation.

Felt such a failure.
Anyhow I'll get up and mount
my dear old horse Endeavour—
I'm a little lost, but not down—
And so to sleep—
I hope lots to do tomorrow
But it looks (out of the window) like
Some real wet in the offing.

But finally, May had to admit it was time to retire and on 8 April 1967, her ninetieth year, she jotted 'No. 1968 last cartoon' on a completed strip and some months later the famous gumnuts disappeared from the Australian press.

She was still fiercely independent and, despite a now precarious financial situation, refused to apply for the old age pension which she considered charity. Her property—the land Cecie had chosen so well—was certainly valuable but it was not possible for her to borrow money without a regular income and the returns she received from the royalties on her children's books were insufficient for comfortable living. For someone who had become an Australian legend, whose creations were the companions of generations of Australians, the income May Gibbs received in her lifetime was extremely inequitable. Payments for her newspaper and magazine strips were only a fraction of that paid to male contributors, while much of their work never attained the popularity of her cartoons.

And yet there were still surprises in store. To her relief and pleasure, one arrived in the post. In March 1969 the Commonwealth Literary Fund had granted her a literary pension of $21 a week in recognition of her work in children's literature. It was arranged by a close friend and fellow author, Ruth Trant-Fischer, who had brought the plight of the author to the notice of the Literature Board and the then chairman, Gough Whitlam. With this pension, which she considered not charity but recognition, she was able to live comfortably, for her life was very simple.

Another surprise was an approach from Angus and Robertson for permission to include extracts from *Snugglepot and Cuddlepie* in cheaper full-colour editions for supermarkets. May was in something of a dilemma—she could not supply the art herself and disliked the idea of someone else illustrating her work. Against this there was her business sense and the chance to entertain

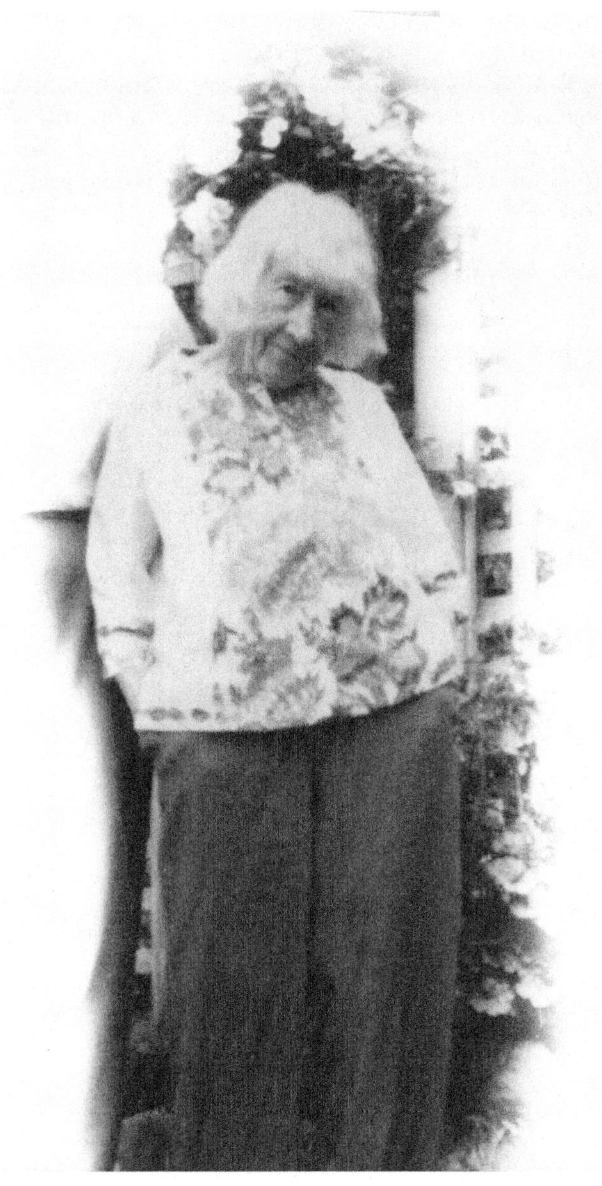

May in 1966. 'I think it doesn't matter how old you are at all, it's just how you feel . . . I wouldn't be able to tell, but I think I'm well over a hundred.'

a wider audience. 'Yes', she agreed but now she *could* insist on quality control.

George Robertson's grandson John Ferguson himself delivered the artwork for the critical scrutiny. He left not only with her approval but with a lasting impression of May's cheerful charm. However, as Eric Marden recalls, 'She wasn't happy with that last book', and this is the impression she left with several friends and relatives, an understandable reaction for a person whose philosophy about her work had always been strongly expressed.

> I had one very decided feeling about doing things, that you must never copy a single line from anyone else, and I hated anyone to copy my work.

Aware of how rapidly she was ageing, May commented in her notebook

This growing old,
Why should we mind it.
We're not afraid of death
Who know so well
How hard it is to give.

There are no dark corners left
Into which we dare not peer,
We know them all, we've dared them,
Swept them out and left them clean.

Time how we value it
And hold it as its time value.
How precious are the little things of life,
Pretence is done
We can afford to be ourselves.

The things we counted big
Have become small and
The little things loom big

This is followed by the criticism:
. . . no good . . . rotten . . . start again!!!!!!
The poet's next line read

We've won a bit and lost a bit
And sinned a bit and hated it . . .

The venerable May Gibbs in many respects resembled one of the small creatures from her cartoons—heavy featured, prominent nose, wiry white hair and a deep voice which still boomed when she did not approve of something Eric had done in the garden. Although there were many attempts to interview or photograph her—for she was a senior citizen of considerable note—she refused.

She was a naturally shy person but there was a more important reason which she explained to one of her publisher's representatives.

> Everyone has an image of their favourite storyteller. It may be their mother, favourite aunt or admired school teacher. I don't suppose two people have a similar idea of me and the thought intrigues me. I want them to keep their favourite idea.

She was still keeping faith with the children.

During a Sydney store promotion of the gumnuts in 1968, she did have fun with the journalists in revealing her attitude to age.

> I think it doesn't matter how old you are at all, it's just how you feel. People have got into the way of saying, 'Oh, I'm such-and-such an age, I don't do this and I can't do that.' I never thought about my age, I just didn't worry about birthdays, so honestly I wouldn't be able to tell, but I think I'm well over a hundred.

She was then ninety-one and had outlived all of her contemporaries. Yet her cheerfulness and her interest in life, no matter that its physical boundaries were those of her garden, never deserted her.

> Dearest Beatrice
>
> The cold weather and house work!!! which I should not have to worry about (but can never seem to shake free of) [May began in a letter to Beatrice Davis]. There's always a lack of help in [the] house—I like to find I have things to do in the garden—but in the house NO! but there it always is brooms chasing me about dust always everywhere 'Woman's work is never done' how true. I do all I can think of to make my house work attractive. I made a lovely apple tart (or pie) and I *can.*

> I have my own special way (I invented it) of making apple tart (or pie) and truly it comes so scrumptious—no one goes past it—Butcher, Baker and Candlestick Maker—all stop and take a big slice—even the postman—goes away with a large piece hanging on his underlip. I stew the apples till almost cooked—then I take a big clump of butter and work flour into it till all is absorbed—a tiny pinch of salt—and never any other moisture is needed—try it or do you do it that way?

The letter is undated and unfinished and was forwarded to Beatrice Davis at A & R after May's death. In November 1969 May Gibbs suffered a stroke which necessitated her leaving No. 5 Wallaringa Avenue, Neutral Bay. Two weeks later, on Thursday, 27 November 1969, she died.

The news of her death touched the hearts of all Australians with sadness, for the mention of her name brought memories of childhood favourites to her multitude of admirers.

In accordance with her wishes, she was cremated. There were no flowers by request but a loving hand had laid a sprig of gumleaves on the casket and her ashes were scattered in the rose garden of the Northern Suburbs crematorium, which had received those of her husband, J. O.

May Gibbs left most of her works of art and royalties from all her books to The New South Wales Society for Crippled Children and The Spastic Centre of New South Wales jointly and, with the exception of some small specific legacies, the residue of the estate went to UNICEF (New South Wales). In gratitude UNICEF endowed the Annual May Gibbs Memorial Art Prize for New South Wales school children.

For over fifty years May Gibbs entertained the children of Australia, colouring her cartoons with her homespun philosophy, weaving social and moral comments into her bushland adventures. Children loved the creatures she gave them, in all their guises, readily accepting the nudity, the Banksia Men, the much criticised mispronunciations. In entertaining them, she also led them to a discovery of their Australian setting, the bushland, which had captured her imagination on her arrival in Australia as a small child. Skilfully she used her characters to awake in all her readers a love of nature and an appreciation of all the gumnut heroes, wildflower heroines, banksia villains and bushland animals she brought into their lives.

A tribute at her passing expressed the sentiments of Australia:

> No one will be quite as good. No one will touch such a multitude. May Gibbs is alone in her creative genius. For this reason May Gibbs has gained lasting fame in her own land.

'The Mother of the Gumnuts' must have the last word.

> I've had the greatest pleasure always in thinking of all those little children who enjoyed my books. Everything became alive for me, it was just a fairy tale all the time.

TWO UNPUBLISHED SHORT STORIES

written under the name of H. Randolf Gaiter

SPOTLIGHTS ON GEORGE AND MRS GEORGE AND KITTY'S ANKLES

Mrs George opened one eye and looked at the clock. It was 7 a.m. She pushed the eiderdown away and raised her other ear from the pillow.

'George,' she called, 'are you shaving?'

'No,' George's sleepy voice replied.

'Oh then it *is* the Gardener sweeping the path next door.'

'I thought you said he'd left,' said George.

'Yes, that's what I mean, he wasn't sure; and if he's not going he'll keep an eye on the house while we're away.'

'Hum,' said George. 'Have you decided where we are going?'

'Well, I thought, as we live on the waterside we'd better go inland.'

'Hum,' said George. His wife could see, through the door, the end of his bed with his bare feet sticking out, he liked them so, even in cold weather.

This reminded her about Kitty's ankles.

'You know, dear,' she said, 'if we don't do something about Kitty soon we'll deserve all that's coming to us.'

'What are you talking about?' said George.

'She never meets anybody, or goes anywhere, she's putting on weight. She doesn't try to make the best of herself, and—'

'And,' interrupted George, 'she doesn't pluck her eye-brows, wear crimson claws and blood red lips, and she doesn't get her head up like an old time dame in a Pantomime, with fishing net and bits of ribbon sticking out and about.'

'But darling, a girl has to be reasonably fashionable.'

'Nonsense, Reason and Fashion don't go together now, if ever. A few years ago women wore sensible shoes, now look at 'em, high heels, stilts, in a hot climate like this.'

'It's going to be a tragedy,' continued Mrs George, 'she adores children.'

'Well, granted we should do something, what can we do?'

George was wiggling his toes, a sign that his brain was making an effort.

'Do something—try something—get to it—think out a plan. Say we start with elimination. Why doesn't she attract men?'

'Too darn sensible,' said George, 'and her ankles.'

'Ah, yes, I know, personally, I feel that's the root of it—dresses are so hopelessly short, I mean, what is a poor soul with bandy legs, or knock-knees to do. Kitty's all right, barring her ankles. Of course, slacks and evening frocks—that's one good thing.'

'Yes, one good thing is, a man does know what he's marrying, these days,' said George.

'If we go up country,' began Mrs George.

There was a playful tapping on the miniature knocker attached to the other side of Mrs George's door, and a cheerfully musical voice called 'Tea O!'

'Come in,' called Mrs George.

Kitty came in. Her black eyes glistening with light, smiled straight into her sister-in-law's eyes: her mouth, naturally red, spread widely showing level teeth, her nose slightly tip tilted was in balance with a fine brow from which swept dark brown hair. The whole effect was a charming one of great good humour. The rest of Kitty was rather buxom—strong limbs—long fingered strong hands, a generous make of woman, and with such sturdy ankles.

She wore a bright blue, short sleeved overall, which crossed and tied at the back with a jaunty bow.

'Oh, Kitty darling, thank you. Oh, a letter! Give George the paper, I'll see what this is.' She tore the envelope. 'Goodness, well! What a coincidence!'

Mrs George continued reading to herself, exclaiming at intervals. Kitty stood smiling, but George, always inordinately inquisitive, hurried in, with his hair on end and his pyjamas all crumpled, spilling his tea and asking, 'Who is it? What's up?'

'It's Vi. She's at "Lapping Stone". John's coming down and she wants us to go and help jolly him up, she says he sounds so tired.'

'How is it a coincidence?' asked Kitty.

'We were just wondering where to go,' said George. 'I must overhaul my fishing tackle. Lordy, I hope the little Troutses are good and hungry this time.'

'Kitty dear, you go and get your tea,' said Mrs George.

When the door closed, she looked at George intently.

'Listen, Vi says, "Bring Kitty". Underlines it twice.'

'Think she's scheming?' said George.

'Positive, she's been trying to get John married ever since—'

'Too old,' said George.

'Nonsense,' said Mrs George. 'Kitty would make a perfect old man's darling—and what we shall do without her I can't think. Oh, I do hope the Gardener will be here to keep an eye on the house. Such a nice boy. I told you he pruned all our Roses?'

'I must get another Cockeye Bundy,' murmured George, gazing into his tin of flies.

The enveloping luxury of the old house closed round them. The warm embrace of their Hostess welcomed them, all were kissed and joked with, as she marshalled their comfort, arranged cushions, pushed a footstool, added an ashtray, or gave an order to the quiet maid.

Profusion of flowers, quantities of cocktails, highly flavoured stories, quality not questioned. Lots of noise and laughter.

She was untiring; how she managed to keep her massive proportions so poised upon such high heels and slender feet, was always a puzzle to George.

At the moment he was entirely absorbed, in Major John's expert proposals for tomorrow's fishing.

'Do you fish, Miss Kitty?' The Major turned to her suddenly.

'Oh, yes, but I haven't got a rod.'

'That's splendid—I have two, in fact three, you shall choose. Come and we'll try them now.'

That was the beginning, then it followed swiftly for all to see.

If Kitty and the Major were not fishing together they were partners in Croquet or Tennis or riding together or walking to the shops.

Their Hostess glowed triumphantly; all her good management. Sweet thing, Kitty—and what a lot of money she'd have. Thoroughly deserved it. Extraordinary how they match, both so jolly, and unconventional.

'I must say,' said George, 'the most darned matter of fact courtship I ever looked on at.'

'I give them one more day,' said Mrs George.

'Bet you it's all fixed now,' said George.

After dinner that night, George found Major John in a quiet corner of the verandah, and sat beside him, lit his pipe, and the two silently watched the great white disc of the moon, rising behind a black silhouette of gum trees.

'Now,' thought George, 'he'll spill the beans any moment.'

'Very lovely, isn't she?' remarked the Major. He meant the moon.

'Well, I think so,' said George eagerly, meaning Kitty.

'So pure, so utterly and sublimely cool. Impersonal,' said Major John.

'Absolutely,' agreed George, but added inwardly, 'What an Ass!, A man in love.' A long silence, Major John coughed several times.

George knocked out his pipe—blew hard through the stem, and refilled it.

'George—I want to talk to you about your sister.'

'About Kitty, quite, quite,' said George.

'She insists on my doing it, though I know I'll make a mess of it. The great thing in these affairs is, keep cool, don't jump to conclusions, hear everything first. That's a bad start,' added Major John.

'Not at all,' said George, 'you're doing fine—go on.'

'She's a great little girl—and—as a matter of fact, well, just has me round her little finger. I want to tell you—'

George, always impatient, leapt in. 'I know, old man, you needn't tell me, I'm delighted.'

'Then you know?'

'Of course I do—we all know,' cried George.

'Ah! That's fine.' The Major sighed with relief. 'Now the question is, when can we get them married, they've all had their special leave and he may be off any day. You do agree with marriage first, don't you? A few wonderful days to remember—if—God forbid—he doesn't come back.'

George, pipe in hand, mouth open, was speechless.

'Of course, his job's there for him, after the war—don't worry, he's a fine chap—very smart chap—one of the very best.'

George collected himself. 'May I ask who you're referring to?' he said.

'Then you don't know?' ejaculated the Major.

'No, I'm darned if I do,' said George.

'Oh Blast!' said Major John. Then with emphasis, 'Your sister is going to marry Jim Crawshay—he's managed my place for two years. He's good stuff, fine stuff, Kitty's lucky, and he's lucky.'

'Rot,' exclaimed George hotly. 'She's never met the man. Anyway where has she met him? What are you talking about?'

'I'm talking about the Gardener who weeds the weeds, and mows the lawn, for your little old ladies next door, who is keeping an eye on the house for you, who came in and pruned all your Roses for the love of doing it.'

The Major threw back his head, and laughed till he almost choked. He mopped his own face and looked at George's. It was a mingle of hurt incredulity and curiosity.

'What's he in?' he blurted.

'Air Force,' said Major John.

'Where did they meet?'

'He saw her getting into a tram; hopped on and followed her home; found next door was a Guest House; found they needed a Gardener; took the job and spent his leave—pruning your Roses!'

Major John laughed again till he nearly exploded.

'How could a man be such an Ass?' growled George. 'Getting into a tram, only her back visible.'

'Says he fell in love with her ankles,' roared the Major.

VERY LITTLE SMALL OLD BOOK

George was browsing along the shelves of a Secondhand Book Shop, sniffing pleasurably the old musty leather, and humming a happy little tune in his neck, for he loved Secondhand Book Shops.

Suddenly, he stooped low, and picked up from a heap of Books on the floor, a very little small old Book. The Brown leather cover was frayed, and the leaves yellow with age. It bore the title *How to Treat a Bad Temper.*

George was enchanted. He read, 'If the Husband has a bad temper, do nothing to enrage the poor soul. Do not say things likely to upset him. If the Creature likes praise, give it praise. If it likes good things to eat, such as Cake and Pudding, Pancakes and the like see to it that the larder lacks nothing that may soothe his mind. If he takes delight in telling of funny stories—encourage the telling—laugh at them each time more and more, in order to hide the endurance and boredom thereof ... The Creature with a bad temper must be humoured, cajoled and cosseted.'

And so the little Book went on, telling all those with Good tempers how to endure with patience the unfortunate souls with Bad tempers.

George knew he had a bad temper, and his delight at finding the little Old Book was immense. He smiled as he read, and looked so happy, that people near, and passing him, felt a curious elation which they could not understand.

As he read, he underlined places with his pencil, and by and by, putting the small, extremely little Book into his pocket, he walked out.

He was so engrossed in his pleasure of the find, that he forgot to pay for it; but he went back next day and did that.

He chuckled all the way home, leaving a wake of happy thought waves behind, so that the boy who sold him a paper, the conductor who clipped his tram ticket, the deckhand on the Ferry, all felt a slightly joyous feeling while the tall man in grey tweeds, with the laughing blue eyes, stood near them.

When he went into his home he looked about for Mrs George. She was in the Garden weeding, he saw her from the bedroom window.

Taking the little, very small Book from his pocket, he went to Mrs George's dressing table and slipped it under her hand mirror. 'She won't be long before she finds that,' he laughed, as he settled himself into a lounge chair, in the cosy-gay Balcony, that looked upon the Harbour.

He read the latest war news awhile, and dozed awhile and then it was Lunch time.

George washed his hands and went in.

Mrs George was looking very fresh in a new flowery overall, and her pink earrings were dancing while she cut bread and served the Macaroni.

'I'll see if she's found the little Book,' thought George, 'I'll pretend to be cross.'

'Macaroni again!' he grunted.

'What d'you mean, again?' said Mrs George briskly. 'We haven't had it for three days.'

'I'd have liked Curry,' grumbled George.

'Nonsense!' said Mrs George, 'the last time we had Curry you said it made your bones ache.'

'I don't remember that,' growled George.

'You said it,' said Mrs George.

'I didn't,' shouted George; he always shouted when he was cross.

'You did,' said Mrs George, glaring at him.

'What!' roared George springing to his feet, 'are you telling me that I'm telling a—a—'

'Yes you are,' said Mrs George springing to her feet.

'How dare you,' bellowed George, his face reddening, his tie flapping, muttering through his clenched teeth; he caught up his plate and flung it to the floor, smashing it to little bits.

'I can do that,' cried Mrs George. She seized the dish of Macaroni and dashed it at George's feet.

George was so astonished, that he couldn't say a word; he just stood there with his mouth wide open, his face slowly turning from pink to pale.

The two black Scotties came out from under the table and licked up the Macaroni from his trousers and the floor.

'I can do lots,' screamed Mrs George. She opened the window with a bang and flung the teapot out, and then the milk jug and the sugar basin, then she kicked over her chair, flung the tea cosy into George's face and went out, banging the door violently behind her.

George was dumbfounded; his legs trembled and his hands shook so that he could scarcely find his pocket handkerchief.

'She couldn't have seen it,' he groaned aloud, 'she must be ill, she must be. What on earth shall I do!'

'Do nuthin', sir,' whispered Mick Gunty, the Gardener, hoarsely, putting his head in at the window. 'Do nuthin', say nuthin',' and he disappeared. George heard him gathering up the broken pieces. He drank a long glass of water, found his hat and went out slowly from the house and garden.

Mrs George watched him go. Suddenly remembering that Mrs Hogarthy must have heard the whole affair, she hurried into the kitchen.

Mrs Hogarthy had been 'Helping' Mrs George for the best part of seven years, each day from nine till four. Her stout figure, quiet efficiency and curiously Madonna-like face were as much a part of the Household as The Georges themselves, almost.

'Oh Lucy!' cried Mrs George, a little flushed and shame-faced but triumphant, 'Thank you, thank you! It worked wonders.' Mrs Hogarthy looked at her in mild surprise.

'How?' she asked. 'What for?'

'For the Little Book,' said Mrs George. 'It's wonderful.'

'Which?' asked Lucy in bewilderment.

'This part,' laughed Mrs George. She put a hand down the front of her dress and fished up the little small old Book. 'This is the part,' she said, 'listen.' She read aloud, 'Now if the Creature with the bad temper does not improve with gentle treatment, then try it with a manner in just the opposite extreme. Be more bad tempered than he, more fierce, do not be afraid, stand to your full height; head up, chin out, and if there are shoutings and smashings, do you likewise, only shout longer and louder, and smash more, much more.'

'There,' said Mrs George. 'I did it, and he turned into a lamb—I could hug him.'

'Don't you, mum!' said old Mick, putting his face just inside the Kitchen door. 'Do nuthin', say nuthin',' he urged, and withdrew.

The truth is George hadn't read all the pages of the very little, old, old Book.

'Of course,' said Mrs George to Mrs Hogarthy, 'it was only the Camping teapot and things that I smashed—I put them there purposely—in case.'

APPENDIX

PUBLISHED MATERIAL

LIST OF PUBLICATIONS WRITTEN AND ILLUSTRATED BY MAY GIBBS

1911 *About Us,* Ernest Nister, London

1916 *Gum-Nut Babies,* Angus & Robertson, Sydney *Gum-Blossom Babies,* Angus & Robertson, Sydney

1917 *Boronia Babies,* Angus & Robertson, Sydney *Flannel Flowers and Other Bush Babies,* Angus & Robertson, Sydney

1918 *Wattle Babies,* Angus & Robertson, Sydney *Tales of Snugglepot and Cuddlepie,* Angus & Robertson, Sydney

1920 *Little Ragged Blossom and More About Snugglepot and Cuddlepie,* Angus & Robertson, Sydney

1921 *Little Obelia and Further Adventures of Ragged Blossom, Snugglepot and Cuddlepie,* Angus & Robertson, Sydney

1923 *The Story of Nuttybud and Nittersing,* Osboldstone & Co. Pty Ltd, Melbourne

1924 *Two Little Gumnuts — Chucklebud and Wunkydoo, Their Strange Adventures,* Osboldstone & Co. Pty Ltd, Melbourne

1929 Small paperback versions with fewer illustrations
Snugglepot and Cuddlepie
Little Ragged Blossom
Little Obelia
Nuttybub and Nittersing
Two Little Gumnuts — Chucklebud and Wunkydoo
All published by Angus and Robertson, Sydney, under the imprint Cornstalk Publishing Co.

1932 *Nuttybub and Nittersing* (re-released), Angus & Robertson, Sydney *Chucklebud and Wunkydoo* (re-released), Angus & Robertson, Sydney

1940 *The Complete Adventures of Snugglepot and Cuddlepie* (combining *Snugglepot and Cuddlepie, Little Ragged Blossom* and *Little Obelia*), Angus & Robertson, Sydney

1941 *Scotty in Gumnut Land,* Angus & Robertson, Sydney

1943 *Mr and Mrs Bear and Friends,* Angus & Robertson, Sydney

1953 *Prince Dande Lion,* Ure Smith, Sydney

LIST OF PUBLICATIONS ILLUSTRATED BY MAY GIBBS

1912 *The Struggle with the Crown, 1603–1715,* Wilmot Buxton, George Harrap & Co., London
Barons and Kings, 1215–1485, Estelle Ross, George Harrap & Co., London

1913 *Georgian England,* Susan Cunnington, George Harrap & Co., London

1913 *Scribbling Sue,* Amy Eleanor Mack, Angus & Robertson, Sydney *A Little Bush Poppy,* Edith Graham, Angus & Robertson, Sydney

1914 *Gem of the Flat,* Constance Mackness, Angus & Robertson, Sydney

LIST OF EDUCATIONAL PUBLICATIONS CONTRIBUTED TO BY MAY GIBBS 1913 TO 1955

Primary Reader Book 1 and Book 2, NSW Department of Education, Sydney
New South Wales Magazine, Sydney
The Outpost Magazine, Blackfriars Correspondence School, Sydney
Mail Way, The Magazine of Primary Correspondence School, Brisbane
Australian Broadcasting Commission programmes

LIST OF CARTOON BOOKS WRITTEN AND ILLUSTRATED BY MAY GIBBS

1925 *Bib and Bub Their Adventures Part 1*, Angus & Robertson, Sydney, under the imprint Cornstalk Publishing Co.
Wee Gumnut Babies Bib and Bub Part 2, Angus & Robertson, Sydney, under the imprint Cornstalk Publishing Co.

1926 *Bib and Bub* (Combined edition), Angus & Robertson, Sydney, under the imprint Cornstalk Publishing Co.

1927 *Further Adventures of Bib and Bub*, Angus & Robertson, Sydney

1928 *More Funny Stories about Old Bib and Bub*, Angus & Robertson, Sydney

1929 *Bib and Bub in Gumnut Town*, Angus & Robertson, Sydney

1932 *Bib and Bub Painting Book*, published by May Gibbs, printed by Penfolds, Sydney

WEEKLY CARTOON STRIPS, WORDS AND PICTURES BY MAY GIBBS

1924–67 'Bib and Bub', total 1968
1925–31 'Tiggy Touchwood', total 331

WEEKLY SHORT STORIES WRITTEN AND ILLUSTRATED BY MAY GIBBS

1925–35 'Gumnut Gossip—Extracts from the *Daily Bark*', total 346

NEWSPAPERS AND MAGAZINES CONTAINING MAY GIBBS ILLUSTRATIONS AND CARTOONS

1889 *West Australian* (children's art competition), Perth

1902	*Social Kodak* (political cartoons, pseudonym 'Blob'), Sydney *West Australian* (fashion illustrations), Perth
1904–09	*Western Mail*, Perth
1911	*Christian Commonwealth,* London *Common Cause* (The Organ of the National Union of Women's Suffrage Societies), London
1913–15	*Sydney Mail*, Sydney *Lone Hand*, Sydney *Tatler,* London
1943	*Bulletin,* Sydney

MAY GIBBS' LEGACY TO CHILDREN AND ADULTS WITH DISABILITIES

Generations of Australians have grown up with her gumnut babies, but the woman who enriched and delighted the lives of so many Australians also left a lasting legacy to thousands of children and adults with disabilities.

Upon her death in 1969, May Gibbs left the copyright of all her works jointly to The NSW Society for Crippled Children (now known as Northcott Disability Services) and The Spastic Centre of New South Wales.

The Spastic Centre of New South Wales and Northcott Disability Services' connection to May Gibbs began when the will of Cecilia May Ossoli Kelly made the following gift: "All my published books manuscripts drawings cartoons works of art (except portraits of my relatives) together with all my copyright therein and all royalties now or hereafter payable in respect thereof to the New South Wales Society for Crippled Children and the Spastic Centre Queen Street Mosman, equally".

One of the most substantial bequests to Northcott Disability Services and The Spastic Centre of New South Wales has been from the designs of May Gibbs bush characters, Snugglepot and Cuddlepie. Northcott Disability Services and The Spastic Centre of New South Wales have long relied on estates and bequests to provide services for children and adults with disabilities and the generosity of May Gibbs will continue to assist them. Her legacy to people with physical disabilities lives on and will continue to do so in the future.

Through her foresight, May Gibbs has assisted thousands of children and adults with disabilities and their families across NSW. Northcott Disability Services provides support and services to over 6000 children and adults with disabilities and their families across NSW and the ACT, while The Spastic Centre of New South Wales provides support and services for children and adults with cerebral palsy from more than 70 sites throughout NSW and the ACT.

Northcott Disability Services and The Spastic Centre of New South Wales are considered leaders in their field of support and service provision to children and adults with disabilities and their families.

The Spastic Centre of New South Wales
http://www.thespasticcentre.org.au/

Northcott Disability Services
http://www.northcott.com.au/

NUTCOTE

5 Wallaringa Avenue, Neutral Bay

The preservation of May Gibbs' home Nutcote, built in 1925, is a story of love and dedication by fans and admirers for an Australian icon.

When May Gibbs died, she left Nutcote to UNICEF who, because of its charter, sold it.

A proposal by Maureen Walsh for listing on the National Trust was made in 1977 and in 1978 Nutcote was properly recorded on the National Trust. This was supported by the North Sydney Council who listed Nutcote in their Register of Significant Homes. All this while The May Gibbs Foundation (1987), headed by Marian and Neil Shand and friends John and Helen Wood discovered the challenge to preserve Australian history. Everyone thinks it is a great idea to preserve our past, then, there are those who actually do it.

Nutcote Trust replaced The Foundation and supporters in their tens of thousands from every state and territory in Australia and its cousin New Zealand, contributed their expertise and money to realise Nutcote's survival for May.

Money problems were ever present and the stalwarts' efforts were rewarded during May's birth month, January, in 1990; when Roslyn Crichton, Mayor of North Sydney, and her councillors came to the rescue and wiped the purchase debt of the house.

The workers, although collapsed in a mental heap, faced the new challenge of keeping their precious landmark alive. God bless, you all know who you are.

Nutcote is still there! Make sure it is on your 'must see' list when in Sydney. All the volunteers would love to see you especially Yvonne, the current editor of the Nutcote News.

Good Root! Go to Nutcote and tell your May Gibbs story.

Ph: 61 2 9953 4453 www.maygibbs.com.au
Nutcote Trust

AN INTERVIEW WITH MAY GIBBS

An Interview with May Gibbs is one of the good things that happened for May Gibbs' devoted followers.

In 1985 *The May Gibbs Collection* was a very successful release for publisher, estate and author. When Maureen received her cheque she went back to her original project 'the feature film'. Without the restraints of money 'the film' began a new development. Maureen edited Hazel de Berg's 1968 interview with May, and May told her own stories matched with stills from generous owners and artistic creations from Herbert Gibbs and May.

Animator, Cam Ford and Maureen worked with a special technique, lighting each piece of art to display the colours and brush strokes used. Marian Shand lent her knowledge of May's life story and Jenny Ochse lovingly photographed the material. Optical & Graphic produced the titles and stills.

James Easton matched the action with his musical talents; Gary O'Grady, sound editor, developed a bush scene and Peter Fenton mixed the sounds for a superlative sound track. Christine Rowell applied her post production techniques and the film still occupies a corner of her life.

Nothing but the best for May! The end result shot on 35mm colour film came to life for its first screening at the Dendy Theatre Martin Place Sydney 1986 when Cam Ford's single animated gumnut slid down a gumtree branch and took a stage bow—one of May's gumnuts came to life.

The film, entered into 1987 International Film and Television Festival of New York, against 5000 other entries, won a third prize bronze in biography.

An interview with May Gibbs sits in most Australian school libraries, has a Japanese language version, was screened around theatres in Australia, released on SBS for a period and launched new projects for those in love with May. Each day Nutcote opens its doors, May Gibbs has an ideal venue for her story.

INDEX

Printed in Great Britain
by Amazon

77940452R00119